Architectural Houses 01

architecture and interior design of houses

Architectural Houses 01

atrium
international

AUTHOR	Francisco Asensio Cerver
PUBLISHING DIRECTOR	Paco Asensio
PROJECT COORDINATOR	Carolina Gallego García
PROOFREADING	Amber Ockrassa
GRAPHIC DESIGN	Mireia Casanovas Soley

PHOTOGRAPHERS Friedrich Busam (*Inhabitable architectural sculpture*); Federico Bonetti (*The Villa Carminati*); Mark Darley (*The Winton guest house, Schnabel House*); Julie Philipps (*Opposing vertical and horizontal planes*); Bossien (*Ritz House*); Francesc Tur (*Ritz House, Bernasconi House*); Filippo Simonetti (*Bernasconi House*); Studio Azzurro (*Single famliy dwelling*); Eduard Mueber (*House in Montagnola*); Timothy Hursley (*Inverted perspective*); Reiner Blunk (*Interplay of symmetries, architecture open to its surroundings, an enriching autonomous construction*), Ferran Freixa (*Absolute fusion*); R. Bryant/Arcaid (*Solid architecture in red concrete*); María Gorbeña (*Landscape in the leading role*), Eugeni Pons (*Private house in Colera*)

© FRANCISCO ASENSIO CERVER, 1996

REGISTERED OFFICE Ganduxer 115, 08022 Barcelona
Tel. (93) 418 49 10
Fax. (93) 211 81 39

ISBN 84-8185-029-2 (complete collection)
ISBN 84-8185-030-6 (volume 01)

Dep. Leg.: 11.198

Printed in Spain

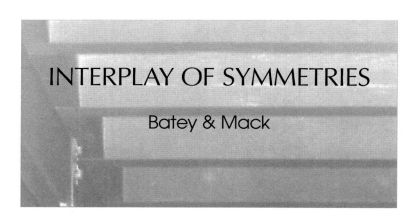

INTERPLAY OF SYMMETRIES

Batey & Mack

Perspective of the cross-corridor showing the wooden ceiling, the dark tiled floor and the light blue columns.

This 3,400 square foot single-family house is set atop a small madrone-covered hill overlooking author Jack London's retreat in the Valley of the Moon. The house is located in Napa Valley, Glen Ellen, California, USA. Seen from the base of the hill, the house stands out clearly against the green of the abundant vegetation because of the colours of the materials used and its strategic and solitary location.

The house was designed by the architect Mark Mack, of Batey & Mack, a company based in San Francisco, in collaboration with Bruce Tomb. Mack was born in Judenburg, Austria in 1949 and studied at the Technische Hochschule in Graz. He continued his studies at the Academy of Fine Arts in Vienna and worked in various firms until he set up his own practice. In 1978 he went into partnership with Andrew Batey and founded *Archetype Magazine*: *During the period of our collaboration, Batey and I had a sort of informal agreement about the way of discovering formal and expressive approaches of our work.* He has been visiting professor in various universities in Europe and North America giving classes at the most important universities in the United States. Since 1986 he has held the position of Associate Professor of Architecture at the University of California. The Knipschild residence has won various prizes including the Progressive Architecture 1984 Design Citation and the Sonoma League for Historic Preservation 1986 Award for Excellence.

The symmetrical, southern elevation is rose-tinted, solid, and compact, concealing an airy, spacious interior. The two seemingly detached volumes are joined on the outside by a concrete

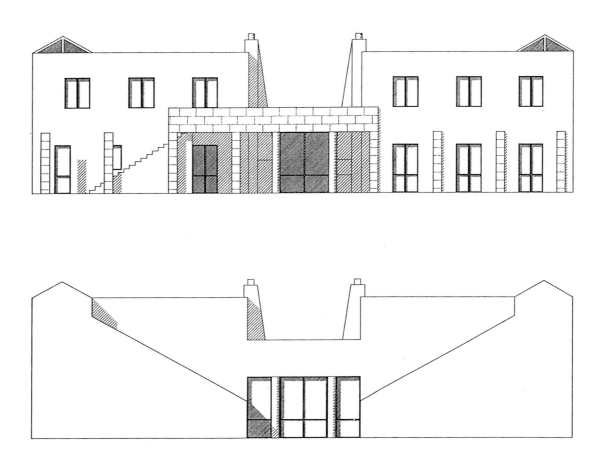

View of the terrace and the lap pool, which sits on a plinth. The blue of the water in the pool harmonizes with the colours of the thick supporting columns.

The material used on the outside is basically concrete and slate. The structural system is a stud wall construction over slab on grade.

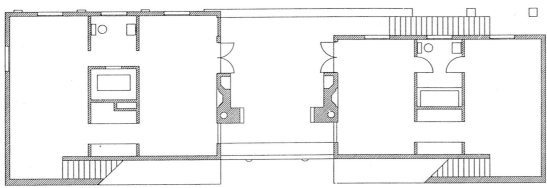

View of one of the units on the south facade showing the linking structure and the steps leading down to the pool.

Panoramic view of the swimming pool and landscape seen from the covered porch through the two thick support columns.

Detail of the south facade, the exterior staircase and the rectangular concrete column.

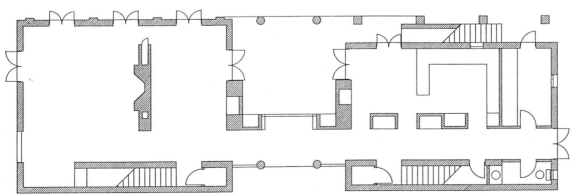

View of the structure that links the two sides on the north facade and contains the front door to the building.

The front door in the central part of the north facade is flanked by two columns which frame the glass door.

structure supported by sky-blue columns, and inside the house they are connected by a cross-corridor. All the spaces have large windows and door saffording wide views. There is also a terrace with a lap pool which sits on a plinth and forms a border between man-made and natural environment. This boundary is echoed in the use of the light blue columns to create a living area open to the exterior and the landscape.

The northern side is a very closed design: the mass and solidity are heightened by the absence of openings in the walls. The entrance to the house is in the central space flanked by two sky-blue columns which frame the glass door. Thus, the two facades are counterpoised: the southern elevation is open to the views and light while the northern side is closed and compact.

The basic materials used in the building are concrete, slate, and metal in the entry. The structural system is a stud wall construction over slab on grade.

The interior is spacious and opens towards the south. The two volumes are connected by a cross-corridor, and each one has a staircase leading up to the second floor. A very simple device has been used to unify the layout: the two upper portions are shared with individual stairs, represented on the outside, forming the entry. As you pass through it, and the view opens up, a kind of gallery forms a secondary axis.

The reception area is in the center of the lower floor. On one side of this area there is a living room-dining room separated by a fireplace, with the kitchen and utility area situated on the other side. All these rooms are linked to the pond and terrace. The pink tones of the living room give it a soft and intimate air.

As mentioned above, in each volume a staircase leads to the upper floor where a terrace separates the master bedroom and

The north elevation is quite closed and has the form of the wings of a butterfly. The volume and solidity of the construction is emphasized by the absence of openings.

Perspective of the exterior concrete staircase on the south facade on one of the two volumes leading to the first floor terrace.

View of the rose-tinted, symmetrical facade facing south, separated into two units connected by a concrete structure with light blue columns.

All the rooms open onto the terrace. The rose color on the walls of the living room creates an intimate and soft ambience.

library from the guest quarters. The staircases are plastered, and carpeted in some areas, and the metal banisters are painted grey.

This single-family dwelling stands out against the surrounding vegetation because of the colors and materials used: for example the rose-tinted facades and sky-blue columns. The design displays a daring symmetry in the glass elevation and a perfect equilibrium in the closed and compact frontage. Inside the house the two structures are connected by a cross-corridor and each has its own stairway leading to the upper floor, where a terrace separates the different areas. The design is complemented by a harmonious classical decorative scheme which makes good use of natural light.

Terrace on the upper level with concrete floor, reached by an exterior staircase.

The two seemingly detached volumes are connected on the inside by a cross-corridor.

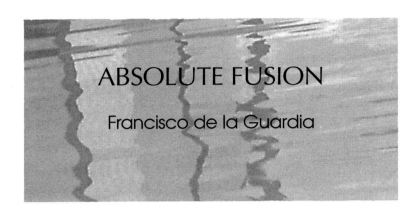

ABSOLUTE FUSION

Francisco de la Guardia

View of the terrace by the swimming pool with the summer dining area.

Using the traditional materials of the island of Ibiza, Francisco de la Guardia has created a work which respects the privacy of the individual, where enjoyment of this marvelous landscape is not only a privilege but an absolutely palpable reality.

This house is located on the island of Ibiza, in the heart of the Mediterranean, situated on a hill from which there is a magnificent view of the sea. The volumes of this work have been faithfully adapted to the slope of the terrain, for which reason all of the rooms and living areas are constructed on different levels.

Francisco de la Guardia was born in Barcelona in 1929. He studied architecture and obtained a doctorate in 1964. His professional career started in 1957 in Morocco, where he was appointed municipal architect in Xauen. In 1959, he returned to Spain and founded an architectural practice in partnership with four other architects: Juan Antonio Ballesteros, Juan Carlos Cardenal, Pedro Llimona and Javier Ruiz Vallés (1958-1959). Since 1984 he has carried out his professional activities alone. He was teaching assistant (1960-1964), course director (1964-1968) and subsequently Department Head (1964-1972) of the course "Projects 1" in the Escuela Técnica Superior de Arquitectura in Barcelona. He has worked as an architectural design consultant for Olivetti (1969-1975), and is the author of a large number of projects and constructions, including single-family dwellings and apartment blocks, schools, offices, banks, clinics and even tourist and industrial constructions. He is in charge of various urban planning projects in Catalonia and the Balearic Islands, and has won a number of awards and competitions.

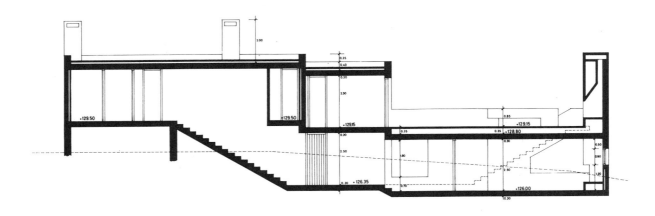

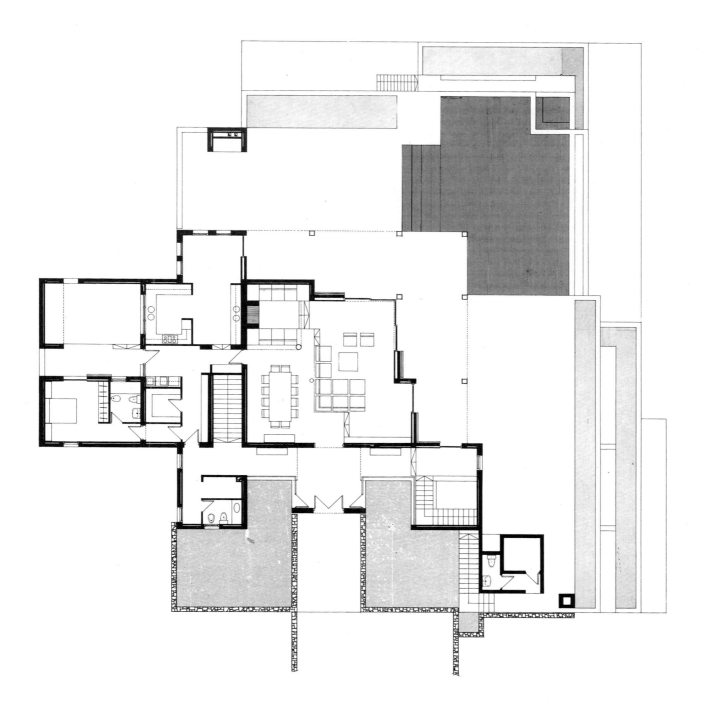

The terrace solarium is paved with tufa flagstones. The blue water of the swimming pool that dominates the southern side blend with the azure tones of the sea and sky.

Section of the house.

This house has been constructed on three levels. The main access to the building, for both pedestrians and vehicles, is on the upper or main level (elevation-0.00). It is composed of a large hall, and two spacious patio gardens, which give access to the four main areas of the house, the living and dining area, the service area, the library-study and the bedrooms, as well as an area for guests. The second two areas are at an elevation of -3.00 and are next to the garage, the service entrance, the machine rooms and the cellar. The service area is in the northern part of the house, and is composed of a double bedroom with bath-

Two stone walls completely delimit the principal access to the house The Wooden door is framed in a square white wall.

Plan of the bedrooms.

Differents sections of the house.

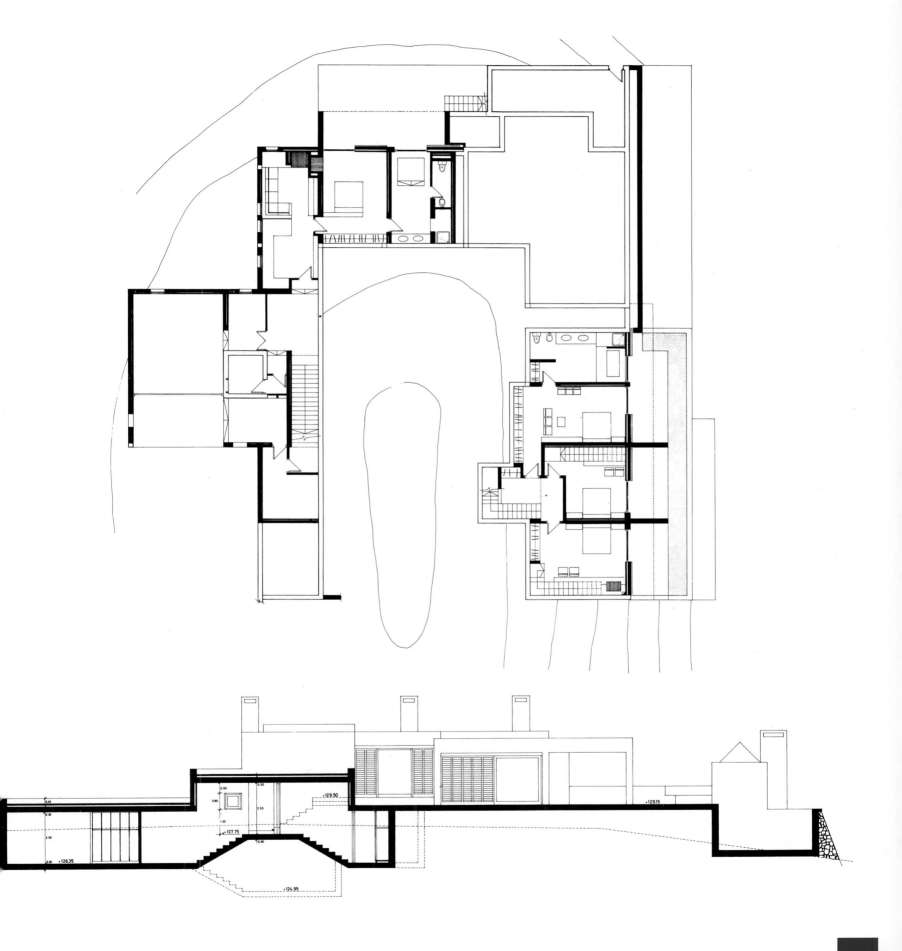

room, and a kitchen-dining room which opens onto the main terrace which surrounds the whole building. From this terrace, one may enter the sauna, showers and bathrooms. There is a large swimming pool in this recreational area which dominates the back of the house.

The abundance of natural light on this Mediterranean island was one of the main determining factors in this work by Francisco de la Guardia. The architect has created two large patio-gardens, architectural elements which allow a maximum of sunlight to be captured. This is why the other openings in the walls (in the form of square windows) are relatively small.

The architect's intention was to ensure the privacy of the dwelling with the construction of a stone wall which totally encloses the main access. Due to the privileged situation of the site, however, from the inside the house is open to the landscape by way of the large terraces and other openings on the south side. The blue waters of the immense swimming pool which dominates the southern facade blend with the azure tones of sea and sky in almost absolute fusion. The resulting effect is a sensation of unrealness and spaciousness.

The desire to root the building in the island and its immediate surroundings is reflected in the use of indigenous construction materials. The beams and arches are concrete. Dry stone walls have been used in the patios, terrace and garden areas, but the interior and exterior walls of the construction have been plastered. The floors and walls in the bathrooms are tiled with local

The glass opening can be covered with lattice screens which protect the interior from the strong sun of the Balearic Islands.

Panoramic view of the veranda, which acts as an intermediate area also serves as an antechamber to the house.

Perspective of the veranda and a detail of the Melés pine doors and window frames.

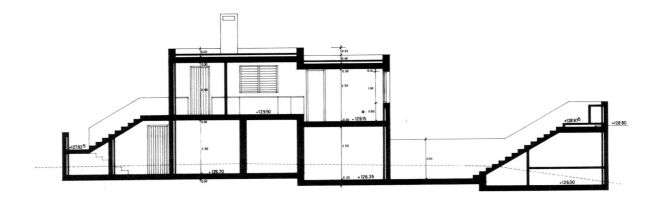

white marble. The carpentry, in pine wood from Melés, has a natural finish which has been used for all of the doors in both the exterior walls and the built-in wardrobes.

There is also a close relationship between the exterior and the interior of this building. The interior patios are the most obvious nexus: the glass walls reflect the colors of the garden so the vegetation becomes the protagonist. Another pivotal feature is the porch, which is also the antechamber of the dwelling. There is a series of materials which are used repeatedly throughout the house such as, for example, the 40 X 40 tufa flooring, which is used outside on the terraces and inside as well, except in the bathrooms.

The interior decoration of this house was designed entirely by the architect. The fireplaces, for example, are one of the most interesting decorative pieces created by de la Guardia: the plain construction material treated with a mortar coat.

As an energy-saving device, this design uses the sun as the principal source of energy through the use of a series of panels which are perfectly oriented and incorporated into the architecture. Heating is provided by means of serpentine elements under the floor throughout the building.

Hidden in the heart of intensely green, exuberant and dense vegetation, this building by Francisco de la Guardia has two distinct facets: on the one hand it is capable of merging totally into the surrounding landscape and achieving almost complete fusion with the sea, taking advantage of the sunlight and its possibilities, thanks to its privileged situation and some of the particular characteristics of the design. On the other hand, it serves as a retreat, offering a degree of peace and privacy which are truly enviable.

View of the white walls of the house. On the left, the stone wall surrounding the house.

Section of the house.

Small square windows with wood frames decorate and illuminate the living area.

The architect was also responsible for the interior design. Light colors and open spaces in the living room-dining room.

Master bedroom with carpeted floor. The woden doors of the wardrobe feature the same decorative motif used in the exterior.

The bathroom has been decorated with local white marble, on the floors and ceiling. The same wooden door is also used in this room to soften the light.

The fireplaces are decorative pieces designed by De La Guardia. They are built into the walls and finished with a rendering coat.

Section of the house.

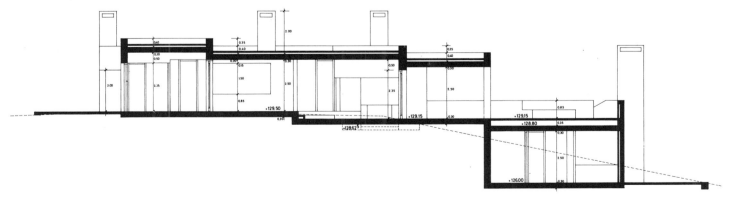

AN ENRICHING AUTONOMOUS CONSTRUCTION

Mark Mack, de Batey & Mack

The roofing, the galvanised iron chimneys, the ligneous facing material and the extremely subtle embedded windows combine to emphasise the character of the upper section.

Capturing a location with an enviable view of its surroundings presented Mark Mack with a no less enviable plot of land on which to carry out an investigation into the unequal shapes which form the basis of this work, in this case the quest for more dynamic combinations from an architectural commission which is constructionalist and monumental, but on a rather modest scale.

This single-family dwelling, squeezed in against the northwest corner of a site at the tip of the Wolfback Mountain Range in California, opens out to a stunning landscape providing simultaneous views of the Pacific Ocean, the neighboring town of Sausalito and the San Francisco Bay, clearly marked out by the huge orange-colored Golden Gate Bridge, which looms up behind a nearby hill framing the rooftops of the agreeable city below. It must, beyond any shadow of a doubt, be extremely gratifying to get up in the morning and look out on this kind of scenery, letting one's gaze sweep round in a 180 degree arc, all the more so since the surroundings include trees and meadows. There is also a back patio full of green hillocks which seem to stretch out to infinity. They are, in fact, part of the state-owned Headlands- which merge in the distance into the Pacific Ocean. Paradoxically, this earthly paradise lies only fifteen minutes from the city. The site is located on a slight slope and the terrain is irregular and rocky.

Mark Mack was born in Judenburg, Austria, in 1949. He studied architecture in the higher Technical School in Graz and later at the Academy of Fine Arts in Vienna. During this period he

worked for Steiger & Partners in Zurich and for Hans Hollein in Vienna. He graduated in 1973, and in the course of that same year travelled to the United States to work with Hausrucker and Emilio Ambasz in New York. Later he moved to the area around the San Francisco Bay, where he worked as an architect. In 1976 he founded Western Addition, an organization specializing in elitist architecture. 1978 saw the beggining of his association with Andrew Batey and the publication of *Archetype Magazine*, of which he was co-founder and director. Finally in 1984 he opened his own architecture studio. Mark Mack has been a guest lecturer in several teaching centers around Europe and North America, he has taught at the most prestigious American universities and since 1986 he has held the post of Associate Professor of

This two storey structure was built on an irregular, slightly arched ground plan.

The rear elevation resembles an impressive grey stuccoed monolith.

The house has been arranged as a light, transparent, autonomous structure.

View of the rear elevation and the stairway. The grey colour of the faca-de is only broken by two windows built into the structure and by the yellow door to the living room.

The smoked glass panels within the latticework glass typical of this archi-tect's windows also help to protect the interior.

Inside and outside the dwelling, the walls have been treated with greay stucco.

Architecture at the University of California.

This dwelling, constructed on an irregular, slightly arched site, is two stories high. The different rooms within the house, in accordance with their function, are divided between the north side, the public part of the dwelling, a huge section which is closed off and whose size is exaggerated by the chamfered frames of the windows, and the south side or private section, which is open and diaphanous, with large windows and terraces for full enjoyment of the dramatic views of the bay and of the Pacific Ocean.

Moreover, the internal areas are arranged on both floors around the chimney. On the ground floor there is a cubicle around this chimney leading to the bathroom; the centerpiece thus obtained makes a natural separation between lounge and dining room. The kitchen is located beside the dining room and slips back out of line with the general facade, trying to transform itself into a small terrace overlooking the real terrace belonging to the area immediately below. The family areas are thus concentrated on the lower floor, whilst the lounge and the dining room/kitchen, which are used more frequently, are on the floor above. Another lower unit attached to the wall houses the garage.

Rejecting strident volumetric mountings and strong coloring hiding walls and column (The architectural preferences of Frank Gehry and Luís Barragán, respectively) and overcoming classical planimetric design inculcated in the architect from his European training, for this structure Mark Mack chose, a unitary shape which includes in the ground plan a kind of wedge coming out of a curved link wall (the back section, facing north, following the road behind the bedrooms) cutting short the edge of the vertex, its rectilinear facade pointing down at the slope. The resultant shape is thrust into the sloping terrain and appears as a kind of modelled rock on the top of the hill. An extremely effective variation on architecture by complexes vouches for this morphological, unitary montage. The curved side of the wall, facing the road, resembles a grey stuccoed monolith, whose surface is broken with subtlety by two built-in windows and the yellow door of the lounge. It is flanked by a recess divided into square panels, only half of whose surface is opaque, thanks to a scale drawing, and from here emerges a suspended outside ladder made of galvanized iron, reminiscent of the emergency ladders which can be seen everywhere in urban America.

The treatment for the front elevation facing the landscape is completely different: the full grey of the back section turns over the facade and changes into a powerful plinth with three door/windows, allowing the area on the upper floor to look out

onto a large terrace. The socle supports the upper floor and is surrounded by a series of large recesses, occasionally interrupted by yellowish wooden sections. In this way the house is arranged as an autonomous piece of architecture, light and transparent. The roof and the galvanized iron chimneys, the coal-like material used for the facings, the subtle and necessary built-in windows– all these features unite to highlight the character of the upper floor in its guise as provisional addition, an agreeable observatory in which to live, surrounded by the view on all sides.

Faithful to the wishes of the owner, Mark Mack altered a conventional double pitch roof (a distinctive feature of the teachings of Laugier decking the edges with corrugated metal. Then,

Interior view of the kitchen, flooded by light through its large windows.

Inside view of the bathroom. The shower area is sealed off by a translucent glass partition.

Terrace leading to the kitchen and a dinning room. The woodwork on the doors is painted yellow.

enlarging all the recesses, he deliberately exaggerated the thickness of the curved facade (already lengthened in order to comply with the necessary 40 foot setback to the west). The smoked glass panels within the trellises which are typical of this architect's windows help to protect the interior. This careful camouflage, together with a deliberately intimidating cement stairway, also help to keep the curiosity of strangers at bay. Nevertheless the main door, painted bright yellow, hints at the exuberant atmosphere in side the dwelling, an impression which is confirmed when the visitor walks in and immediately discovers that the architect has created an interior house which nonetheless stretches outs, graceful and mature, towards its surroundings.

Realizing that the agreeable bedrooms, sundrenched in winter, could be transformed into unbearable ovens during the summer months, Mark Mack builtirradiated heat floors which, when they reach a temperature higher than that permitted by the thermostat, automatically activate a water circulation system which progressively cools the cement surfaces.

Inside the house, Mark Mack's primitivist tendencies are to be found in the wooden furniture which he himself designed, and also in the red stucco chimney. The decision to include built -in stereo speakers was not the result of aesthetic or acoustic considerations, but rather the dimensions of the chimney. Even so, the consequent asymmetry fits in well with the rest of the house. Inside the building, the walls have been treated with grey stucco, as they have on the outside; the stone floor hides the built-in panel heating; likewise, the wood is of a yellowish colour.

Mark Mack has built this house with the client's wishes and the idiosyncrasies of the location very much in mind. The result is the expression of irregular angles which nevertheless express themselves as directly functional. This dwelling does not wish to be confused, either due to its shape or its material content, with the surrounding landscape. At the same time it wishes to be a part of that same landscape in a creative manner, however, shunning crude mimicry. It is thus an individual creation, separate and autonomous, enriching this composition of complex elements, conquering the best of two contrasting worlds, the comforts of city life and nature in its most uncontaminated form.

View of the bedroom with grey stucco hearth.

Interior view of the glass facades and the yellow wooden doors.

THE WINTON RESIDENCE GUEST HOUSE

Frank O. Gehry

Partial view of the house.

Among the most original and innovative contemporary architects in the USA, Frank O. Gehry is one of the most significant and admired in the world. He is also a central figure in the L.A. art scene and his extensive work embraces a wide variety of creative disciplines. However, as often happens to those who surprise and perplex their contemporaries, until a few years ago Gehry's work had not been understood, at least by the general public. Only now after many of his projects have achieved widespread critical acclaim has he begun to be known as one of the most important figures in the architectural avant-garde.

Gehry's architecture is based on his own language, a synthesis of numerous different influences, such as postmodernism and deconstructivism, combined with a very personal conception in which we can see his liking for curved lines, the recurrent use of certain materials, and a tendency to create several independent volumes which, complement each other, achieving pure and schematic compositions. All of this is modulated by his powerful fascination for the energy and chaos of the city of Los Angeles, a city with which he has particularly close ties.

The Winton Residence Guest House, a modest building designed by Gehry in 1987 to complement the main residence, is a very significant example of his work because it allowed him to put into practice some very interesting ideas which until then had only been theories. The result is one of the best balanced and most serene constructions by Gehry, who seems to have left behind the tensions present in many of the projects he designed

General view of this spectacular house designed by Frank O.Gehry.

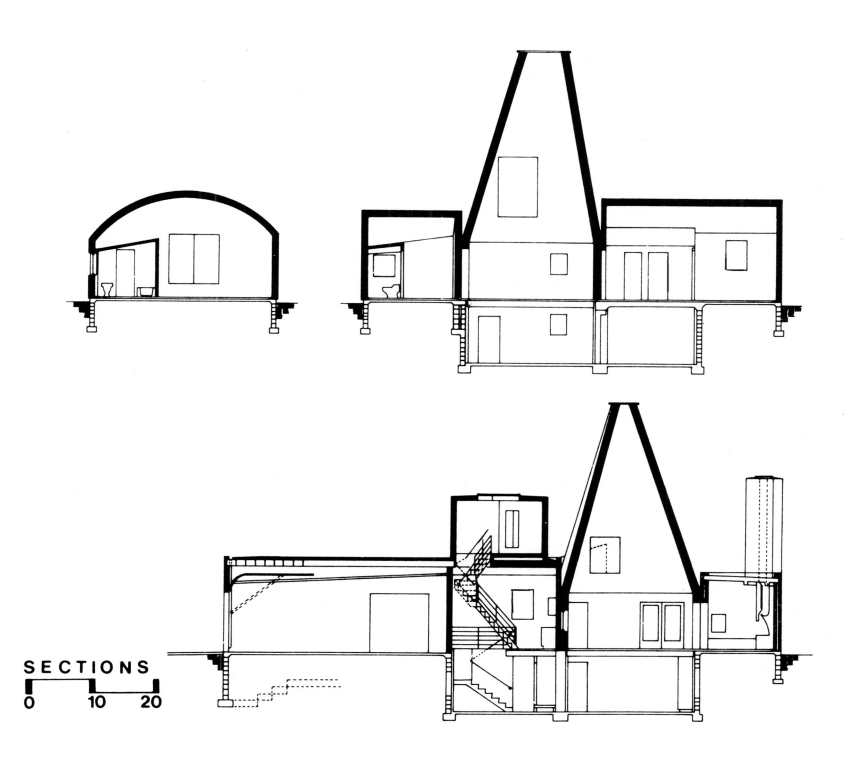

SECTIONS

0   10   20

Sections of the Guest House.

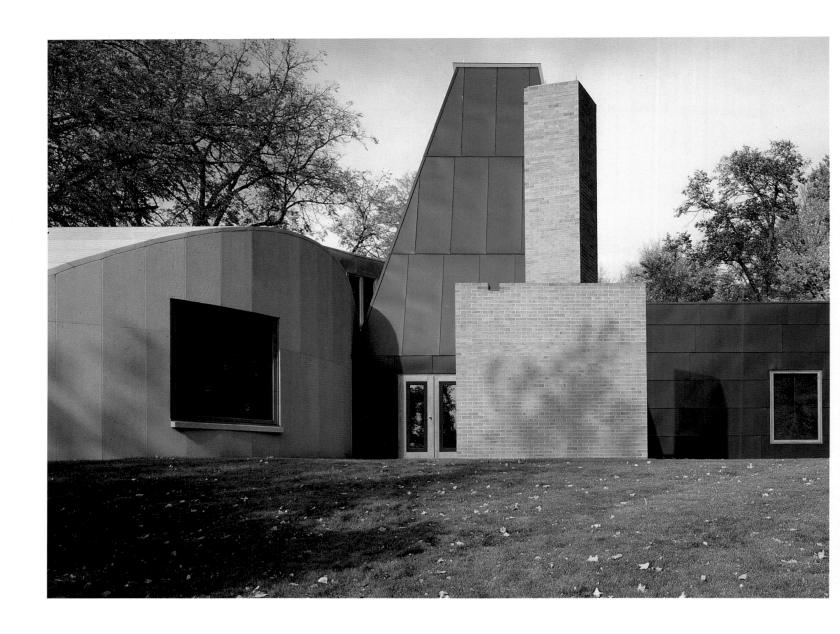

Two views of the main facade.

during the seventies. This interesting trajectory has brought him to these pure and personal forms, the fruit of the creative maturity of this artist.

Frank O. Gehry was born in Toronto, Canada in 1929 but moved to California at an early age. He studied architecture at the University of Southern California from 1949 until he graduated in 1951. He completed his formal training at Harvard University, where he took a course in City Planning. For the next few years he worked with a number of prestigious architects such as Victor Gruen in Los Angeles (1953-1954), Hideo Sasaki in Boston (1957), Pereira and Luckman in Los Angeles (1957-1958) and André Remondet in Paris (1961). In 1962, he established his own firm, Frank O. Gehry and Associates. It was not until 1978, after he completed his own residence in Santa Monica (Los Angeles),

that his work gained more general recognition in the contemporary architectural scene. Since then he has been commissioned to design and build increasingly more important buildings all over the world (Los Angeles, Japan, Paris), and his work has made him one of the most acclaimed architects in the world. Gehry was named 1989 Laureate of the Pritzker Architecture Prize, considered to be the most prestigious award for architectural achievement presented to a living architect.

Frank Gehry's achievement has also been demonstrated in his many other activities, such as teaching which has played an important part in his career. He was Assistant Professor at the University of Southern California from 1972-73 and from 1988-89 at the University of California at Los Angeles (UCLA). He has also been Visiting Critic at Rice University (1976), UCLA (1977 and

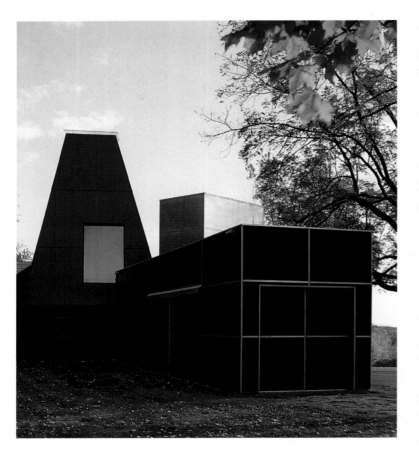

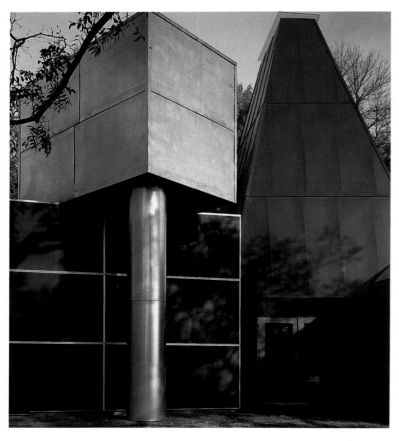

1979) and Harvard (1983). In 1986, he was honored by the Los Angeles Chapter of the AIA for his outstanding contributions to the chapter and the profession. In 1987, he was made a Fellow of the American Academy and Institute of Arts and Letters and has received honorary doctoral degrees from the California Institute for the Arts, the Rhode Island School of Design and the University of Southern California. His work has been the subject of many exhibitions, has been featured in major publications and books and has regularly been the subject of seminars, debates and conferences.

In this project, the architect above all had to pay particular attention to the existing main residence on the property: an essentially rationalist, unified and transparent work by Philip Johnson. In the design for the new guest house these formal characteristics had to be taken into account. Although Gehry was free to choose any style he wished for the new construction, it had to respect the setting and not disrupt the inherent personality of the property. The house is located in a heavily wooded area on a hillside beside a large lake in a suburban area roughly thirty miles from Minneapolis, Minnesota. The client wanted a modest building which would maintain the sense of the natural landscape and complement the formal qualities of the existing main house.

The building, which is a guest house used by the children and grandchildren of the owners, is broken down into a series of one-room buildings which together resemble a large sculpture set on the lawn. The nucleus of the construction is a large truncated cone that rises up in the centre of the ensemble and houses the living room. Five more one-room units cluster around the cone, each one displaying different shapes and colors and executed with different materials. On the northwest facade, there is an elongated rectangular bow shape which houses the garage and kitchen. Opposite this, an irregularly-shaped building with one curved side and a vaulted roof contains one of the bedrooms inside a cube-shaped block crowned by a span roof. The fourth building is smaller and contains the fireplace alcove off the central sitting room. Finally, the third bedroom or sleeping loft, situated over the kitchen in the service wing, is a cube partly suspended in the air and partly resting on a cylindrical column.

Thus, the different pieces in the ensemble are linked together and enrich each other in a sculptural collage. The disparity of textures, materials and colors creates an attractive visual impact. Gehry likes to establish links between the forms and the materials, and for this reason he often uses surprising materials in order to emphasize the form of the one-room buildings which are a feature of many of his projects. The central tower of the Winton

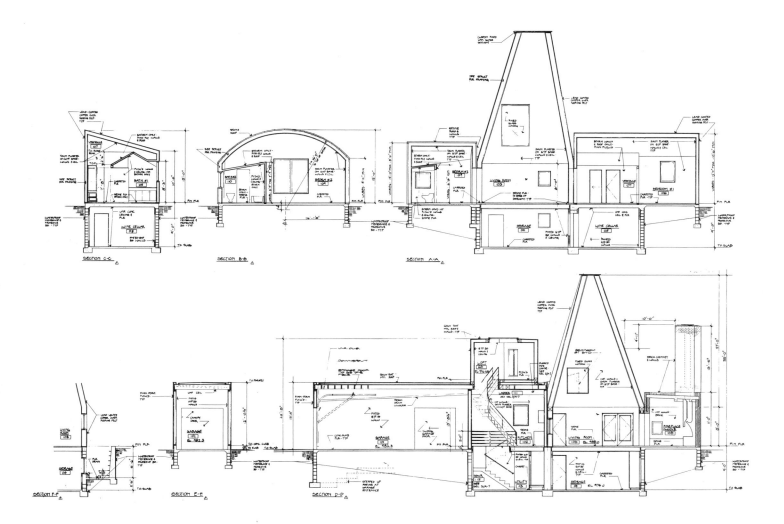

Guest House is a wooden structure sheathed with metal panels painted in two colors: a dark slate grey and a copper tone. The box-like service wing, on the other hand, is covered with finn-ply, a prefinished plywood. The curved bedroom is clad with kasota, a local dolomite limestone, giving this volume a pale colour. The other bedroom, like the living room, is sheathed with dark, almost black, painted metal panels. The shiny grey sleeping loft perched on the edge of the service wing is an unpainted, gal-vanized metal structure, and the fireplace alcove is a brick cube topped by a brickwork chimney.

There are very few windows in the walls of the buildings and those included are irregularly-shaped and designed without ref-erence to scale. They are distributed randomly throughout the house, appearing high up or low down on the walls or in the roof. They capture fragmentary images of the surrounding landscape. Intense light enters from all sides creating an interesting interplay of light and shade. The interiors give a sense of openness gener-ated by the flow of one room into another and the splendid views of the surrounding garden.

Another of the formal caprices of this work is the staircase leading up to the sleeping loft. The underside is encased in unfin-

Details of the structure.

Longitudinal sections of the Guest House.

47

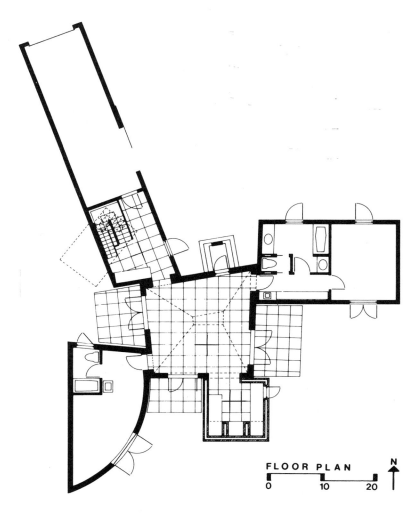

FLOOR PLAN

0   10   20

N

ished wood and wire glass clearly visible from the ground floor. This detail was requested by the clients and is a reference to the controversial "deconstructed" style made famous by Gehry in the seventies.

One of the features of this work is that, given the formal conception, it can be enlarged to accommodate the changing needs of the owners whenever necessary. This brings us to one of the constants of Gehry's work, the unfinished appearance of his buildings. His projects often appear to have been mysteriously abandoned during the construction process. However, this sensation of fragility and impermanence which is a characteristic of his work is absolutely intentional. This desire to create a feeling of transience seems to spring from the fact that the architect's final objective is not the permanence or completeness of his project, but rather his desire to transcend this feeling and create a work of art.

The new Winton Residence Guest House is an attractive response by Frank O. Gehry to the aesthetic of the main house designed by Philip Johnson in the early fifties. This was achieved using his own very personal style to create a masterpiece which reveals the new and exciting possibilities of architecture in the twenty-first century.

Plan showing the six one-room buildings which make up the house.

All the rooms in the house can be accessed from this central living area.

Detail of the compact closed volume which houses the intimate fireplace alcove.

Detail of the staircase leading to the sleeping loft, a reference to Gehry's "deconstructed" style.

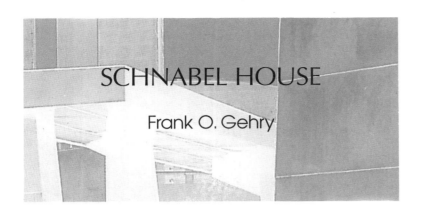

SCHNABEL HOUSE

Frank O. Gehry

The interplay of reflections, planes and perspectives is one of the most expressive elements of this design.

In order to appreciate the creative universe of Frank O. Gehry it is necessary to understand a number of factors which affect his designs for houses in a very special way, factors such as his choice since the beginning of his career of a particular area (California), his efforts to provide a solution to some very specific social needs, and his acceptance of the limitations imposed by modem production systems. This Canadian architect is considered to be one of the proponents of impoverished technology, advocating the use of low cost, industrially manufactured materials (chain link, corrugated cardboard and metal siding).

Frank O. Gehry was born in Toronto, Canada in 1929 but moved to California at an early age. He studied architecture at the University of Southern California from 1949 until he graduated in 1951. He completed his formal training at Harvard University, where he took a course in City Planning. For the nest few years he worked with a number of prestigious architects such as Victor Guen in Los Angeles (1953-1954), Hideo Sasaki in Boston (1957), Pereira and Luckman in Los Angeles (1957-1958) and André Remondet in Paris (1961). In 1962, he established his own firm Frank O. Gehry and Associates. It was not until 1978, after he completed his own residence in Santa Monica (Los Angeles), that his work gained more general recognition in the contemporary architectural scene. Since then he has been commissioned to design and build increasingly more important buildings all over the world (Los Angeles, Japan, Paris), and his work has made him

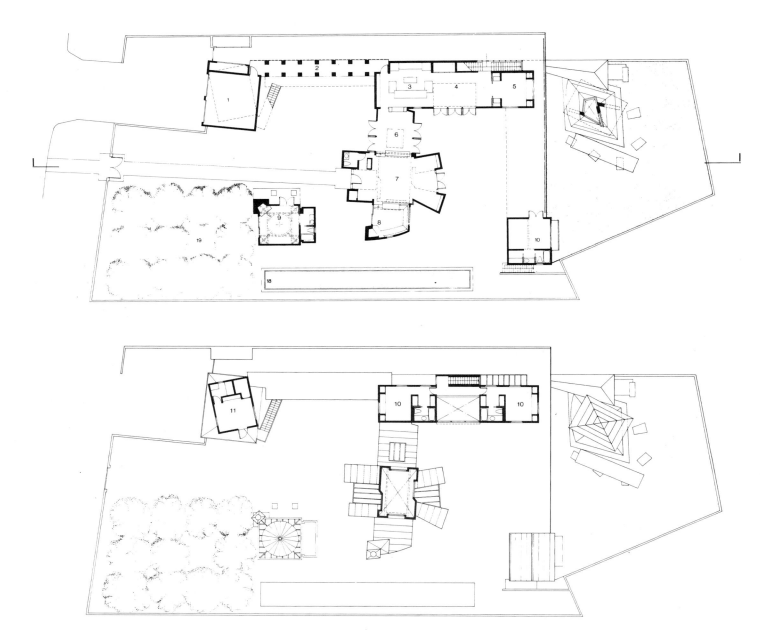

one of the most acclaimed architects in the world. Gehry was named 1989 Laureate of the Pritzker Architecture Prize, considered to be the most prestigious award for architectural achievement presented to a living architect.

One of the most famous examples of Gehry's work in the field of domestic architecture is the Schnabel Residence in Brentwood (Los Angeles). The construction of this building was started in July 1987 and it took almost two years to complete. The building's unusual morphology and atypical typology and the surprising choice of materials were made possible by the comprehension of the clients, who were more concerned with the cultural, aesthetic and pragmatic aspects of the process of habitation than by any mindless submission to conventional mores and general trends in domestic architecture.

Plan of the first floor and the roofs.

Plan of the lower level showing the artificial lake.

View of the front of the main block.

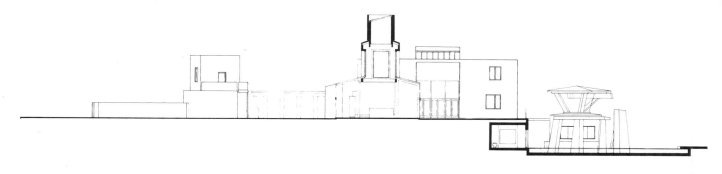

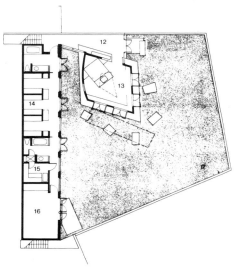

General plan showing the layout of the different constructions.

General view of the Schnabel Residence taken from the rear of the property.

The artificial treatment of the water and vegetation is an integral part of the conceptual atmosphere sought by the architect.

The site selected was a property of approximately 530 square meters with no remarkable topographic features. At one end, the roughly rectangular site terminates in an irregular trapezoidal area where the slope was cut back to form a lower, more private terrace. The absence of significant external conditioning factors meant that the architect enjoyed total liberty and could design the project using the site to the best advantage.

The architect responded to the elaborate building program (private, service, and leisure areas in addition to garage and outdoor installations), with a solution based on independent structures, treating some of the different program elements as distinct objects. This relationship extends into the conceptual and aesthetic sphere. By changing both the shape and surface, each of these buildings (laid out in a wide two-level garden) is infused with its own specific architectural style, and the objects are played against each other in a tense and expressive spatial and sculptural dialogue.

Once this close connection between building and function has been explained, it is possible to trace a natural route through the different blocks in this composition. Due to the geographic orientation this itinerary runs west to east.

Attached to the northern side of this cruciform element is a two-story building housing a variety of rooms. The kitchen is situated on the ground floor of this rectangular structure (closely connected to the main dining room), and at the center there is a double-height skylit family room. The ground floor plan is completed by a small study. The upper floor contains two bedrooms with *en suite* bathrooms. This block has been finished on the outside with a simple grey stucco used to create an intentional visual austerity which contrasts with the artificiality of the lead finish on the adjacent block.

In the entrance area on the west side of the property connected to the street, a small stucco box has been constructed to house the garage. A smaller structure, which has been placed on top of this and rotated at an angle, contains the staff living quarters. Gehry has designed an arcade supported by pillars clad in natural copper, which crosses the garden to link this building to a door into the kitchen. The focal point of the eastern part of the property is a shallow lake which echoes the trapezoidal shape of this end of the site and provides a charming setting for the more private areas of the house. This is the area where the slope was cut back in order to form a lower, more private terrace, and to improve the views from the rest of the site. It is also the site of two other structures of inescapable architectural interest.

View of the glazed entrance taken from inside the house.

The living room in the cruciform building is flooded with natural light.

View of the main bedroom showing the unusual rhomboidal sky-light window.

INHABITABLE ARCHITECTURAL SCULPTURE

Thomas Spiegelhalter

View of the east side showing the ramp providing wheelchair acces.

This unique building is located in the harbour area of Breisach on the Upper Rhine in the southern part of Germany near the French border. It is the realization of a dream, the materialization of this architect's ideas about the way we understand the complex world in which we live. With this architectural sculpture, designed as a place to work and live, Thomas Spiegelhalter has attempted to demonstrate how much we underestimate the complexity of life by trying to express it with an order and organization based entirely on right angles.

The architect of this amazing building, a young German sculptural architect, has taken a stand against the ideas of the media theorists who propose computer generated virtual reality and rejects the reduction of human beings to mere cerebral nervous systems. He strongly believes in direct physical experiences and spaces that actually exist, and suggests that the increase in immaterial and body passive images in our environment produces, as a counter-reaction, a "*radical need for visual, olfactory, tactile and kinetic freedom.*". As this unusual thinker defends reality and corporeality as the irrefutable starting points of all human experience, he firmly believes in the need to go beyond our conventional understanding of reality.

Thomas Spiegelhalter was born in Freiburg in 1959, and received his training as a sculptor in Venice in 1977. He also received a degree in architecture and a diploma in three dimensional visual communication in Bremen, Flensburg and the Hochschule der Künste in Berlin. Since 1991 he has worked in

research and teaching in the department of architecture in the University of Kaiserlautern. His studio and architectural practice is located in Freiburg.

The following is a selection of some of the very interesting work by this sculptural architect and some of the many awards he has received: first prize in the Schinkel Competition in Art and Construction (Mäkisches Viertel, Berlin, 1985-86); design project for Art in the Plaza (Gross-Geray, 1986); first prize in the international competition for an urban planning project for the Berlin wall: Wall of Ice, the Aesthetics of Disappearance (Berlin, 1987); second prize in the competition Art in Construction, for the expansion of the federal administration building (Greiburg, 1988); Westend-Komplexbrigade, an installation on the railroad land around the Artists' Station of the Hofer Society (Berlin, 1988); Logo-Motiv, a special citation in the competition for an urban plan for the city of Weil am Rhein (1989); Jamith, installation in the Schwarzes Kloster municipal gallery (Freiburg, 1990); the Karl-Hofer prize for the project Gravel-pit Architecture (1990); Fischwärts project for an exposition in the Still und Bruch gallery (Berlin, 1991); honorable mention in the competition for the head offices of the Residual Waters Company in Breisauger Bucht (1991); low-cost reform project for an office complex including preliminary study and on-site details (Südbaden 1991); first prize in the competition for the House of the Church, an Evangelical Meeting House (Bad Herrenalb, 1991); and Bioclimatic house (Breisach, 1991).

Spiegelhalter believes that the essential experience of reality lies in heterogeneity, decentralization, and non-standardization as opposed to a design which has been adjusted to provide a coherent whole with an unequivocal meaning. The fundamental principle which fuels Spiegelhalter's architectural credo is that "disturbance" and disorder open the mind, freeing us from the

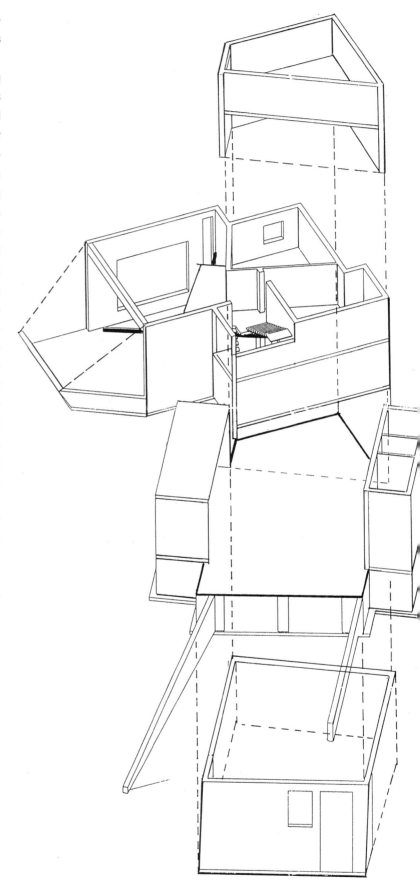

Axonometric plan showing the different volumes in the building.

East elevation.

Plan of the ground floor.

Plan of the upper floor.

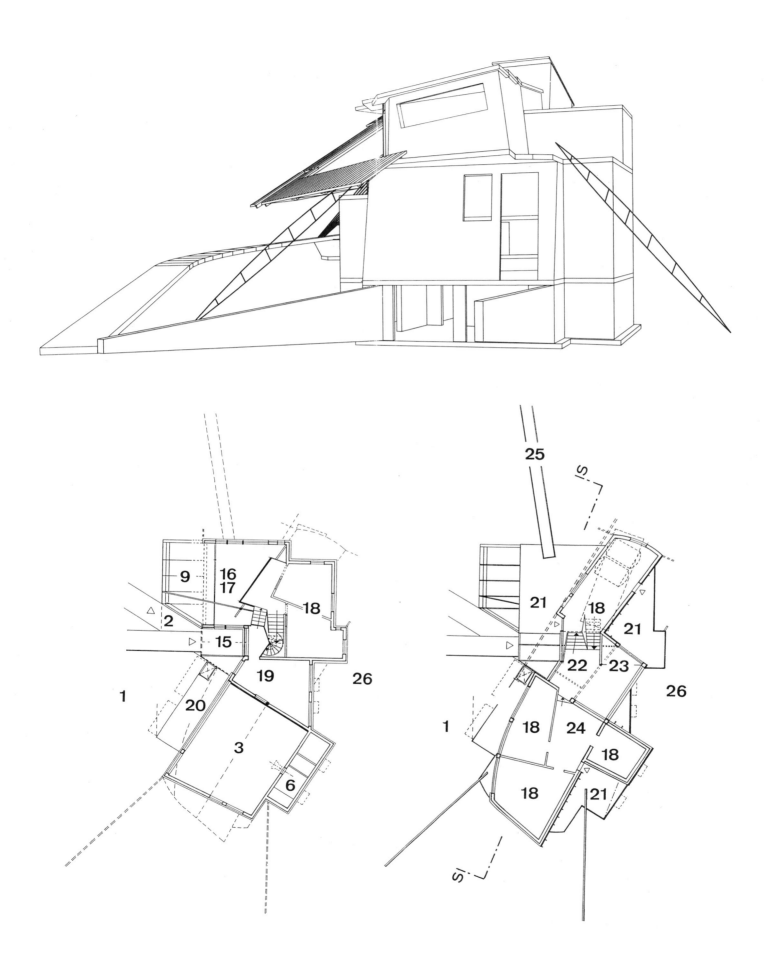

strait-jacket of conventional models with which we try to pin down and fix the chaotic and ever changing manifold of reality.

Spiegelhalter found a rich source of disruptive material in the geometry of the gravel pits which are a common feature of the Upper Rhine industrial belt. In these special microcosms he found what he needed to oppose the static orthogonal systems and implement his ideas of dehierarchization and disfunctionalization. The gravel pits are seen as intermediate landscapes situated in the no-man's land between the natural and the artificial, between the organic and the technical. Their fundamental quality is movement and constant flux. The paradox of the quarry is that it consumes itself and is marked by its own gradual extinction. Nothing in the gravel pit is static of final. The architecture consists of functional structures which from the beginning are flexible and provisional so that they can be dismantled as soon as the work in the pit is completed. The pit is a process rather than a final purpose and it has no result except a supply of raw material. Even the topography of the pits themselves is the random creation of the excavation. Spiegelhalter sees the gravel pits as sites which can be reused as soon as the pit is closed. He proposes building work rooms and flats inside the existing structures and replacing the pit with a pond. This gravel-pit architecture was the main inspiration for the Breisach project carried out in 1992.

After a lengthy period of consultation to decide on a site, a building of 613 m² with a volume of 2127 m² was constructed to house seven inhabitants. The building has a solar energy generator and photovoltaic installation, and contains a media and multi-purpose hall fitted with audiovisual equipment. Recycled material recovered from the gravel pits, transport equipment and junction systems which had been classified unsuitable for

The northeast facade showing the juxtaposition and interpretation of volumes reaching a complicated equilibrium.

Night view of the southeast facade.

The double-height living room on the ground floor is adjacent to the conservatory garden and aquarium.

Interior of the multi-purpose living room showing a small stage at the rear.

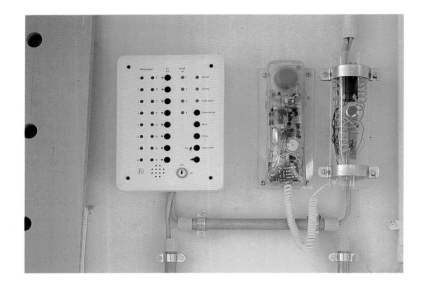

use elsewhere, found a new use in this project. The intrinsic movement of this architectural sculpture, which evokes that of an insect or an excavator is the result of the superimposition of different space complexes and their supporting structure, which optically counterbalances gravity. This is a solitary and dynamic element full of passages, open structures, abrupt breaks, precipitous slopes; a mishmash of theoretically useless fragments and materials coming from other contexts. Thus the house is a portrait of the complexity of the world, a model for the belief that it is not the continuum that is the decisive factor, but the break. Finally it clearly reveals the porosity of the systems which make up our perceived reality.

The kinetic impression thus created is reinforced inside as well as out by the eight roughly interconnected levels and volumes which define the interior. This impression is further heightened by the solar modules on the southern side and the latticework spatial structure on the western facade. The longitudinal glazed facade acts as a thermal shock absorber. Facing south, it is open to the sun and makes the most of the available solar energy throughout the year. The solar generators and collectors are grouped in an organized and integral manner in front of this facade. This equipment fulfills both a functional and aesthetic role, serving as a roof and a gateway into the living space and media center. The oscillating geometry of the solar panels, collectors, heat accumulating water tanks, photovoltaic systems and other ecological technologies contrasts sharply with the cyclical emergence of the plant biotopes covering the facades, structural elements and terraces of the building. The solar collectors and generators, the bathroom, kitchen, rainwater collection system and organic garbage collector form a complete techno-

Detail of interior lighting with exposed cabling.

Transparency is one of the elements which gives order to the composition.

Even the sanitary fittings are used as formal elements.

Interior of the multi-purpose living room and media hall.

artistic ensemble, created through the interpenetration, displacement and juxtaposition of the spatial levels. The entrance hall and stairway are vertical and diagonal voids which penetrate all levels and all volumes. These are connected in turn to the media hall by a steel ramp-bridge, and to the conservatory fitted with specially treated solar glass by a ramp providing access for the disabled. This building was designed as a house and laboratory and is composed of different introverted and extroverted spaces. It not only contains experimental spaces which take advantage of renewable energy and areas for plant cultivation and raising small animals, but also includes transitional spaces intentionally left free for the future.

Technically, the building is constructed around a massive primary structure made of prefabricated concrete slabs which provides highly efficient thermal insulation. The natural rough finish of the brickwork and reinforced concrete is exposed. The wood is

unplanned and the surfaces are a bit marred by wasteful finishing materials, although they are partly varnished like a watercolor painting. The final work is a document of the construction process. The secondary system is composed of light constructive elements taken from gravel pit constructions, and all of the above mentioned technology. The solar energy systems provide hot water and heating (a combustion heater is used as a backup system during long periods without sunlight). Unlike the theoretical architectural works of Peter Eisenmann in which the design can be entirely independent of habitability criteria, Spiegelhalter places the human being in the central role, making him the planner of his own environment. This house provides accommodation and at the same time is open on all sides emphatically inviting contact with the outside. Spiegelhalter's work is the absolute antithesis of the work of architects like Tadao Ando whose houses are designed as protective castles. On the

contrary it is closely related to the work of Bernhard Tschumi in that he pays particular attention to the spaces between the buildings. This young German's architectural ideas are similar in many ways to several other contemporary architects such as Robert Venturi or Frank O. Gehry. But Spiegelhalter draws even more radical conclusions from the chaos typical of modern urban development than even Venturi with his decorated sheds, or the SITE group which, in the seventies, concealed banal functional housing units behind decoratively crumbling facades. Spiegelhalter deals impartially with whatever reality offers him, without trying to order the many impressions by creating a hierarchical structure, seeking rather the broadest possible juxtapositions of all forms of urban reality.

General view of the living room from the upper floor.

The kitchen is composed of a series of functional elements.

A lively colour scheme in the staircase inifies the different planes.

SINGLE FAMILY DWELLING

Franco Stella

View of the central atrium.

This house outside Thiene is one of the most recent of Franco Stella's projects, and it has confirmed his protagonist role on the architectural scene, a result of his language, which is pure, dense and simple but with a remarkable ability to arouse extremely complex reactions. The importance of the plan lies in its calculated transformation of topographical inadequacies to the benefit of a functional distribution that is bold and highly effective. To design a building on the basis of the dichotomy of presence and absence, mass and space, addition and subtraction, is an aesthetic achievement of singular elegance that is complemented by the precise articulation of the structural axes to define the various levels.

His point of departure is the formal and conceptual expression of a serene, isolated, almost timeless space, built without reference to the setting. The Italian architect achieves his objectives, integrating the annexed facilities into the structural composition and granting an unusually prominent role to the lowest level of the building. From the outset, the entire concept of residential design arises from the need to create the best possible living space.

The house was built in the architect's native town of Thiene in the Italian province of Vicenza. The site is located on the outskirts, on a piece of land that is typical of the area, characterized by terracing, an obstacle to the intervention process. The ground plan is nearly rectangular, 45 X 29m² in area, with an irregular slope descending from the Via Santa Rosa.

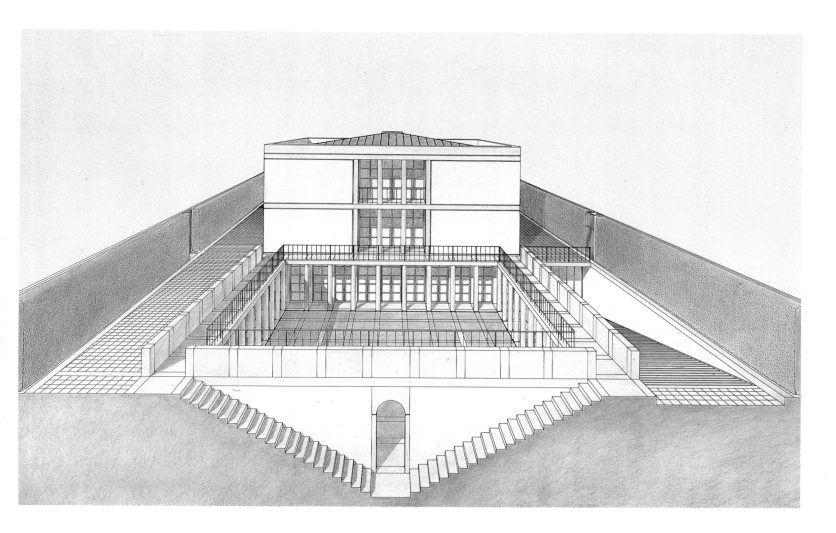

The most rational way to overcome the inconvenience of the terrain was to use the terraces to develop the construction in levels. In this way maximum use is made of the available space, and a perfect distribution of areas is achieved by situating the volume of the house at the highest point, level with the road, and the auxiliary facilities on the lower contour elevation. This building system, frequently used on this type of topography, is the best solution to the problem it poses. However, the architect chose to modify several essential aspects of the basic scheme in order to approach the humanizing concept and the way of life he intended to express with this project.

His premises refer to the attempt to create an autonomous structure, free from any type of influences, whether architectural or of the surrounding environment. This peripheral district is in close touch with nature, and consists of a group of houses built in the conventional repertoire of the second residence. The architect conceived this project as a space that would be independent of its setting but without sacrificing contact with the fresh air and light. Another of his initial objectives was to obtain the nec-

Side view of the atrium showing the columns in detail.

Plan of the house.

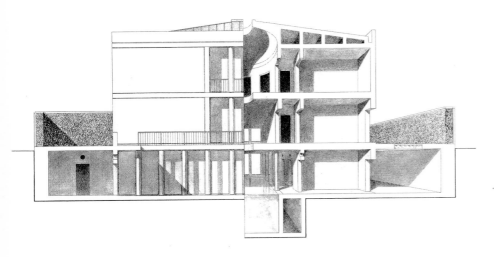

essary privacy both for the interior of the house and for the leisure facilities. All of these goals are aimed at forming an ideal space for the individual – serene, relaxed and close to nature – without resorting to huge glazed openings, a technique employed all too frequently.

To achieve his objectives, the project was distributed in levels but several innovative touches were introduced. The most fundamental was the situation of the residence and its outdoor facilities within the same architectural dimension, without separating them or treating them as independent elements. On the contrary, these plans are fully interrelated as complementary states of a unitary reality. Thus the building becomes a synthesis of two antithetical forms, one addition and one subtraction, with similar quadrangular ground plans. These two sections are interpreted in conventional terms as a three-story house, with two floors above and one below ground level, and a sunken courtyard. This simple description, however, deserves clarification.

The layout, based on the concepts of presence and absence, as well as a strategic adaptation to the topography of the site, is separated from the surrounding estates by a railing and a wall about 3m high to ensure the required degree of privacy. In the space in between them, paved with grey Serena stone and greenery at the entrance, there are various communication systems that connect the floors and the functional areas: a ramp for vehicles that follows the slope of the land and two opposing flights of steps that link the two lower floors with the exterior. Thus the house has a two-fold perspective. From the highest level, that of the Via Santa Rosa, the volume appears as a compact two-story mass, with a double-height central opening of superimposed balconies. From the lower level of the porticoed courtyard, the house appears to have no contact with the setting, as if it were outside of time and space, related only to itself and to the atmospheric environment.

The core living space, the house, has a square ground plan articulated by a central cross that divides the space into four equiangular sections. The functional programe is ordered by levels, situating a specific aspect of domestic life on each plane. Thus the underground floor houses all the sports and personal care facilities. The floor at street level contains the spaces reserved for receptions and house guests, while the top floor accommodates the family areas.

The layout is articulated by the intersection of longitudinal and transversal axes that form a simple cross. On the ground floor, the longitudinal axis takes the form of a vast interior corridor through the building, preceded and terminated by porticos that

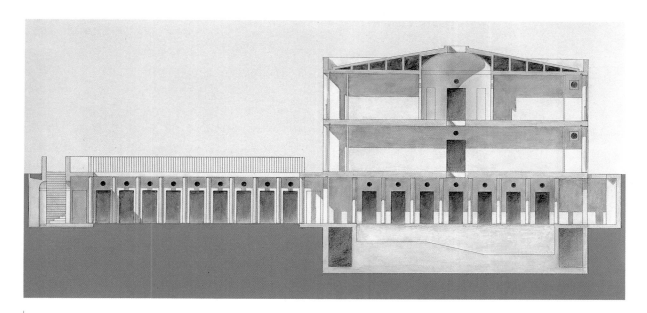

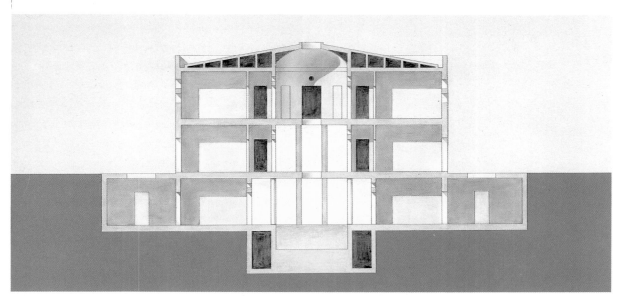

face the street and the courtyard, around which the various rooms are arranged. On the first floor, the imaginary line runs through a space covered by a flat dome, which is connected to all the rooms: the living room and the dining room above the sunken courtyard and the bedrooms facing the Via Santa Rosa. On the underground level, the longitudinal axis orders the columned room of the swimming pool, which has five glazed portals that provide light from the lower courtyard.

Along the transversal line are the hollow spaces containing the vertical communication systems: the stairways and the elevator. One of the most expressive creations of the entire composition is found at the intersection of the two axes: three round openings, 1.20m in diameter, in the floor slabs generate a third

View of one of the entrances.

Two sections of the building.

mode of perception that completes the overall reading of the internal space. They lend a plastic effect that is not only an elegant method of diffusing natural light from the dome, but also forms a symbolic link between the air, the sky and the water.

The external appearance of the building is a symmetrical composition, articulated by two axes. Between the light-coloured walls, the use of white Istria-Orsera stone calls attention to the existence of a central ordering cross. On the street and courtyard facades, the two superimposed balconies framed by blind walls emphasize the longitudinal axis. On the lateral elevations the placement of the windows registers the vertical communication systems. The horizontal pattern of the stone both demarcates the levels and accentuates the crowning dome.

Without a doubt the courtyard on the lowest level is the core of the plan. It is enclosed by a portico of 32 monolithic columns, also executed in white Istria-Orsera stone, and the paving is in teddish porphyry. The walls that enclose it assume different forms on the four facades. At the swimming pool, the wall opens in a row of pilasters, framing the glazing that provides the pool with natural light. The opposite face is more closed so as to emphasize the elegant central arch that communicates with the opposing flights of steps. On the sides are various (XDW) placed doors that open onto the garage and other underground service areas. On the ground floor, four parapets in white stone bound a walkway around the courtyard that leads to the well of the converging flights of steps.

Franco Stella's project might be regarded as a theoretical and practical manual of the building strategies that define his style, which is pure and simple but capable of generating spatial tensions and complex networks of relationships. To build this house near Thiene, Stella has transformed the obstacles inherent in a terraced site into a means of creating an ideal distribution of the functional programe. This is achieved through a composition based on two antithetical forms, addition and subtraction, presence and absence, that define the house itself and the external facilities within the same dimension. A calculated articulation along the two main axes, reflected by the organization of the surfaces, the material treatment and the openings, creates a columned courtyard on the lowest level to fulfill the two basic criteria of the intervention. A classical mood, serene and timeless, governs the complex and attempts to express the ideal space for the individual and for family life.

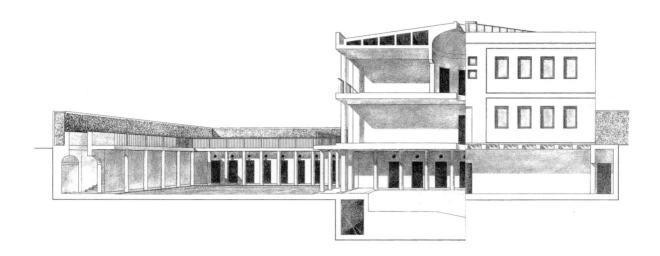

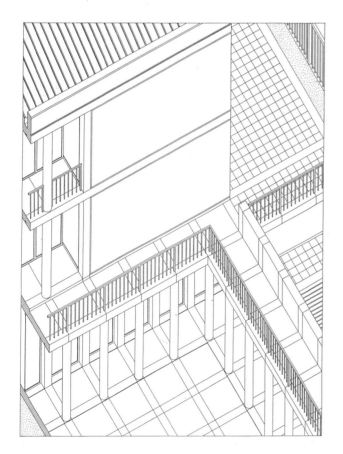

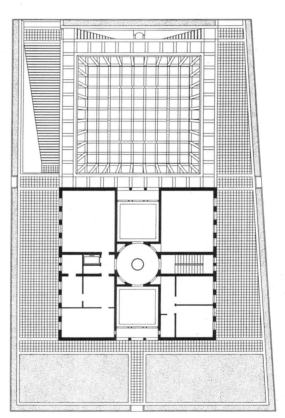

View of the top floor.

The stairs leading to the top floor.

Three different plans of the Villa Carminati.

Next page, views of the swimming pool and aerial view of the atrium.

SOLID ARCHITECTURE IN RED CONCRETE

Claudio Silvestrin

The entrance is through a narrow vertical gap, which leads into a large rectangular patio.

This house on the Spanish island of Mallorca is the first solo work by the Milan architect Claudio Silvestrin, and is one of the most interesting pieces of architecture to appear in the last few years.

The building is situated in an ancient olive grove, part of a property which had belonged to the Neuendorf family for years, only a few kilometers from the busy, tourist traps on the coast of Mallorca. The owner of the house, Hans Neuendorf, is a well-known art gallery owner from Frankfurt. In view of the setting on this part of the island, Neuendorf intended to build a summer residence here which would adapt to the typology of the site. Claudio Silvestrin suggested to him the construction of a minimalist building which would enrich the surroundings into which it was inserted. Thus the Milan architect chose to build a structure which bears no resemblance to traditional Mallorcan architecture, and he may view the results with all the pride of an artist satisfied with his creation.

Claudio Silvestrin was born in Milan in 1955, and initially studied art and philosophy. He became interested in architecture in London at the end of the seventies. He started a business there with John Pawson, and the two men mainly produced designs for single-family dwellings and art galleries and always for an international clientele involved in the world of art. This particular working relationship with the Neuendorf family began in Frankfurt, and Silvestrin carried out this project in Mallorca after parting company with Pawson.

The reddish concrete walls of the building, sober and imposing, are clearly visible from a distance and contrast with the

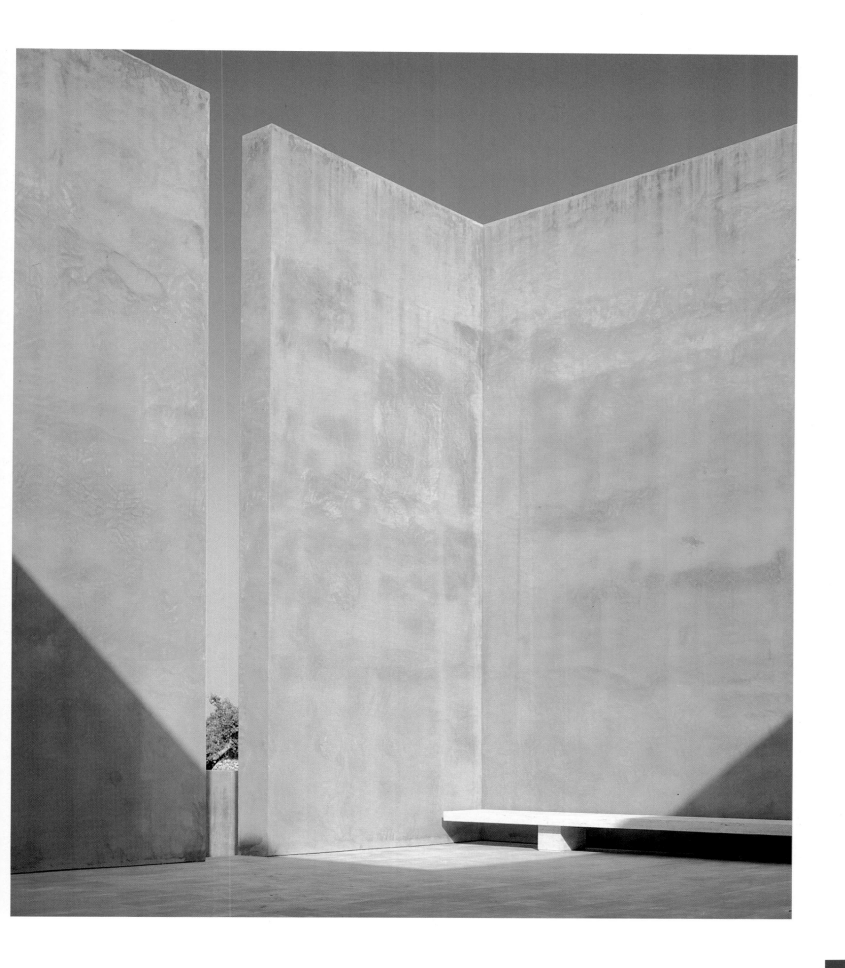

The reddish concrete walls of this building, sober and imposing, are clearly visible from a distance.

General plan.

green of the olive grove and the blue of the Mediterranean sky. The entrance is through a vertical gap in a 9m wall at the end of a 110m flagstone path, enclosed by a wall on one side. The gapleads into a large, practically empty rectangular patio where the only feature is a white stone bench against one wall.

The rectangular swimming pool is at the rear of the house. It is extremely long and has been built on a platform, commanding some marvelous views of the groups of trees which surround the building.

Inside the house, the prevailing ambience is one of clarity and transparency, due to the considerable size of all the rooms and the fact that they all rise upwards or extend sideways in a balanced combination of geometric shapes. The grandiose atmosphere is reminiscent of the tranquility and splendor of a medieval monastery, since the enormous proportions are further accentu-

Detail of the rectangular opening giving access to the house from the swimming pool.

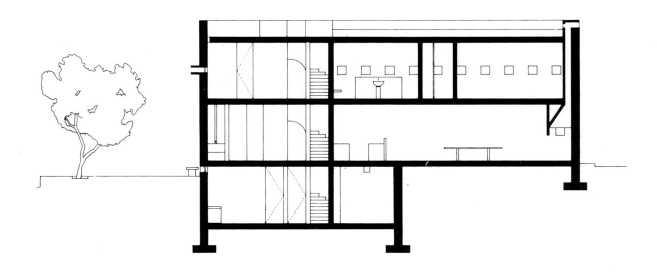

ated by the sparsity of furniture and interior decoration. This effect of total emptiness is in turn accentuated by the eye-catching play of light and shade created by the architect by strategically-placed skylights in the ceiling which let in filtered sunlight. Sunlight strikes the brilliant white of the walls, creating a chiaroscuro contrast which ensures that each and every room is transformed into a work of art.

One of the idiosyncrasies of the Neuendorf residence is the lack of those architectural features considered essential in the construction of a modern dwelling. For instance, it has no

Section showing the different levels of the house.

Views of the swimming pool which is a long, narrow structure adapted to the slope of the land.

entrance door, lounge, kitchen or fireplace. Moreover, the bookshelves are concealed behind a windbreak. In this construction Claudio Silvestrin has adhered strictly to the guidelines of minimalism by including a minimum of features for maximum effect.

The bedrooms were given preferential treatment as areas for rest and relaxation. The master bedroom has two chairs – the only furniture apart from the bed – bathed by the sunlight filtering through an opening in the ceiling. Abundant sunlight shines down diagonally across the white walls to enhance the effect of solitude. In the children's bedroom four tiny square peepholes in the concrete wall allow a partial view of the olive grove against the blue sky. The watchword in every room is simplicity, so that each feature is master of its own space and possesses its own individual identity. The baptismal font design of the washbasin in the bathroom is a clear example of this interplay of space and significance.

The architect wished to escape from typical Mallorcan constructions, and create a house which would constitute a break in the surrounding landscape and dominate this landscape by its very presence. He has nevertheless successfully retained references to the island through his choice of materials. The white porous stone used in almost every section of the house was quarried locally in a nearby village, and the ç on the exterior walls comes from the red earth found locally which provides suitable pigmentation. The sculptural appearance of the exterior provides a counterpoint for the minimalist interior, where the prevailing color scheme consists of the white walls and the yellow porous travertine flooring.

This solid piece of architecture consists of a cold, empty interior which contrasts with the warmth of the reddish outside walls. The Neuendorf summer residence resembles a fortress amid the green of the Mallorcan olive grove, a structure which rejects the traditional style of houses on the island. In spite of the daring design, the first solo effort of Claudio Silvestrin has translated both the wishes of Hans Neuendorf and also his own as a minimalist architect while respecting the surrounding landscape.

View of the narrow vertical entrance. All the rooms are characterised by their absolute simplicity.

The play of light and shade is produced by the strategically-placed skylights in the ceiling, creating diagonal bands of lights across the walls.

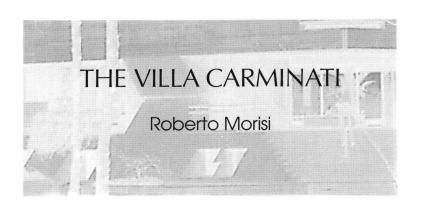

THE VILLA CARMINATI

Roberto Morisi

View of the main facade of the house.

Front elevation characterised by its aggresive volumetry.

The design of private houses offers architects unmatched opportunities to implement unusual, innovative and eclectic ideas. When an architect opts for the unusual, however, the success of the project lies in his skill in combining a pragmatic approach concerned with the quality of life in the house with an atypical, heterodox, and sometimes ambiguous aesthetic. In the Villa Carminati designed by the Venetian architect Roberto Morisi, this combination has been handled very skillfully making it one of the most interesting private residences of recent construction in Italy.

Roberto Morisi was born in Venice in 1926 and obtained his degree in architecture from the University of Venice in 1949. He subsequently moved to Trieste, where he worked as an architect until 1952. He specialized in the use of reinforced concrete at Milan Polytechnic, and in 1956 began work on various projects with Luigi Moretti, Minoletti and d'Olivo. Between 1970 and 1985, he was in charge of many construction projects in Algeria, where he set up a practice with the Milan base company Ingegneri Consulenti. He has also worked extensively in the Far East, the United States, Canada, Germany and Saudi Arabia. Since 1986 he has worked principally in his native country, where the construction industry has been stimulated by the investments of real estate firms and major construction companies.

In recent years he has restricted his work to projects of extremely high architectural quality, mainly in the tertiary sector. His work has been featured in prestigious magazines such as *Domus, L'Architecture d'Aujourd'hui, Architectural Review, L'Industria delle Costruzzioni* and *L'Arca,* and also in books such as *Architettura Italiana* by A. D. Pica and *Les Constructeurs Italiens,* published by ICE.

This residence, built in 1985, is situated on a 1500 m² plot on the outskirts of Canonica D'Adda, a small northern Italian town near Bérgamo in Lombardy. The characteristics of the surroundings which had the most influence on the architect's final design

View of the south-facing rear facade of the house.

were the beauty of the Alpine landscape and the existence of many houses in the vicinity which reflected the traditional architectural vocabulary of the area. The original idea was that the residence should stand out boldly as a powerful piece of architecture and be a very vital composition.

From the point of view of structure, Morisi organized the design into various units. The structure was divided into several levels, creating a vertical construction in which the potential problem of an excessively solid building was, however, avoided by the strategic use of unusual changes in direction with lines veering off at an angle. This created a volume of imposing plasticity, a spectacular composition of geometrical forms which in turn configured the interior layout. The curious organization of the Villa Carminati is largely responsible for the visual impact of the building; it is the key element of the design and exerts an influence on almost all aspects of the composition.

However, Morisi has attempted to soften this digression from the typology of the region by using a number of stylistic and expressive devices; the pale, sober color scheme, the profusion of windows and general transparency of the building, and the insertion of the house into the immediate setting by planting low vegetation and creating a number of ponds around the house. These concessions do not, however, cause the house to lose its forceful visual impact, resulting from the combination of several different volumes, each characterized by straight lines, sharp edges and sloping planes.

One aspect of the Villa Carminati's layout which determines its unusual appearance is the treatment and arrangement of the four floors. The starting point for the design was a semi-basement floor which provides a base for two more floors crowned by an attic. All the floors are perfect squares, but differences in the outline and orientation shape the strange volumetry of this construction.

The semi-basement acts as a socle for the whole building. It rises out of the sloping terrain at an angle, thereby creating a platform for the floors above. The profusion of windows through-

Fragment showing the opposing directions of the different volumes.

Partial view of the entrance.

Night view of the house.

One of the small pools beside the stone staircase leading to the main entrance.

out the house softens the rigidity of the volume, and reflects the importance of natural lighting in the design. This sloping socle was also used to incorporate secondary entrances, in particular the stairway on the north side which provides access to the main floor and is perfectly integrated into the construction as a whole.

On both sides of this stone staircase the architect created two small ponds that encircle part of the perimeter of the building. These ponds are a clever feature providing interesting reflections and visual perspectives. Once above the difference in grade between the ground level and the ground floor, the first totally visible structure features an all-glass entrance set back with respect to the rest of the facade. This entrance is composed of a series of inclined planes and converging angles, which generate forceful aesthetic tension. Here, the use of glass once again serves to soften the rigid geometry of the design.

The positioning of the volume containing the first floor is the structural strategy which has the greatest influence on the appearance of the building. This block has a considerably smaller perimeter than the others and is rotated at a 90° angle to the main axis determining the position of the other floors.

The superimposed top floor, a much more solid and weighty structure than the one below, is the decisive counterpoint in this

The singular composition of the Villa Carminati is one of its main charms.

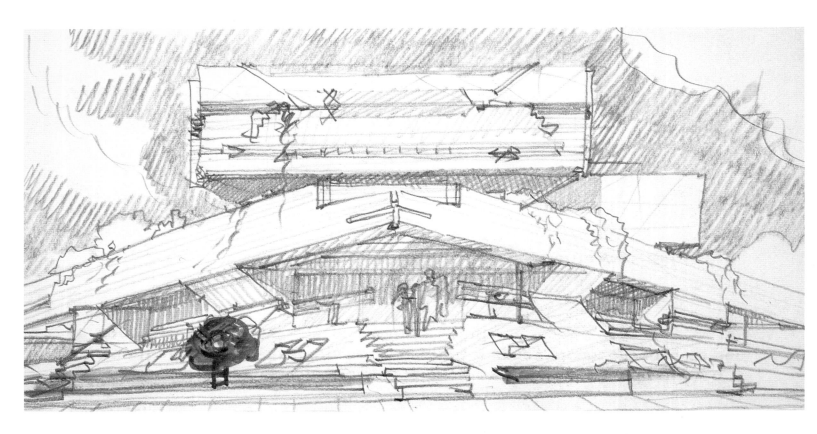

Sketch of the Villa Carminati.

View of one of the side elevations.

Front elevation showing the swimming pool annex.

General plan of the complex.

curious volumetric arrangement. This almost windowless parallelepiped follows the same axis as the ground floor, bringing out the contrast between the arrises and geometric vertices. On the southern facade there is a recreational annex which houses the swimming pool. This metal and glass conservatory structure functions as both an interior and exterior element.

The careful treatment of the materials used on the exterior of the villa reveals the architect's deliberate aim to minimize the aggressive proportions of the building. To this end, he used very natural and elegant materials and an exquisitely delicate color scheme. The exterior appearance of the residence is basically determined by three materials: grey stone, exposed reinforced concrete and travertine stone. The glass walls and windows throughout the house are an essential factor in the basic composition of the dwelling. They under-score the visual relationship between the interior and the surroundings and flood the house with sunlight.

The functional program is laid out on four levels. The semi-basement floor contains the service areas and a gymnasium equipped with sauna and bathroom, a lobby with a bar, a dance floor and a television room which can also be used for showing films. The floor above contains the various family areas in a classical living room/dining room/kitchen layout, and the glass swimming pool annex.

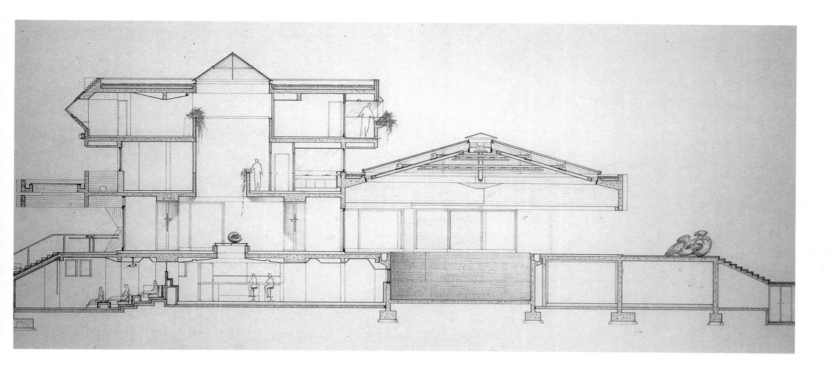

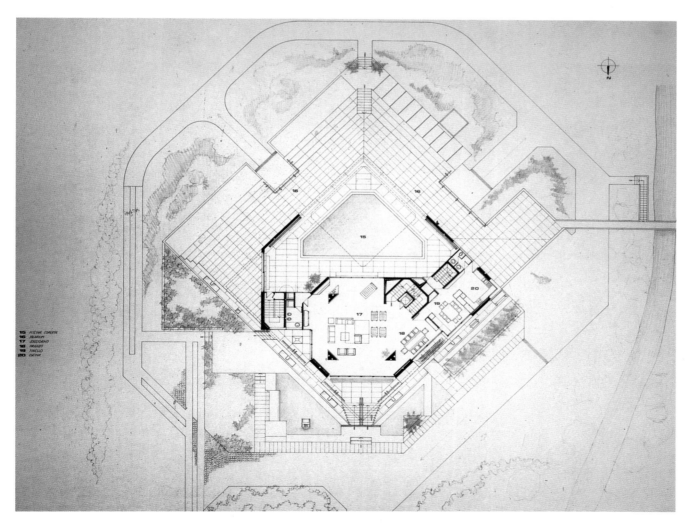

15 PISCINE COPERTA
16 IGIENICO
17 SOGGIORNO
18 PRANZO
19 PASCOLO
20 GIORNI

The design creates an unusually close relationship between interior and exterior.

The swimming pool seen from inside the house.

View from below of the glass roof over the swimming pool.

The carefully planned layout, the use of rich, warm materials, the choice of functional and modern pieces of furniture and the wise use of sunlight create a balanced contrast between an imposing exterior appearance and a cosy interior.

The charming living room occupies part of the ground floor.

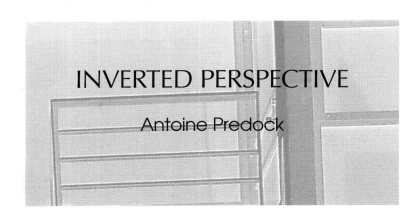

INVERTED PERSPECTIVE

Antoine Predock

The house is built on three floors on a rectangular base.

On an elevated urban site located on Venice Beach in California, USA, Antoine Predock has built an original residence where he has set up a "reverse perspective" view from the inland side of the house. The architect accomplished this trick of inverting the perspective by using a diverging upward-sloping ceiling and a glistening black granite runway on the floor that evokes the sea in the distance.

A beach front promenade is the only thing that separates the house from the beach, lapped by the ocean's waters, so that the occupants enjoy a truly privileged location affording a splendid panoramic view of the Pacific Ocean and other nearby beaches as well as of the city. The house is one of a line of buildings, so that its dimensions, especially the width, are limited by the adjacent houses.

Antoine Predock studied at the University of New Mexico and Columbia University where he received his degree in 1962. He has practiced in his own studio since 1967. Besides his professional activity, he has been active in teaching, as a visiting professor and critic in the most important universities in the USA, including Arizona State University, Harvard University, the Southern California Institute of Architecture and UCLA. In 1981 he was elected to the steering committee of the National Committee on Design of the American Institute of Architects (AIA). His many architectural works can be seen in Arizona, California, Colorado, New Mexico, Nevada and Wyoming. He has also done some landscaping projects in New Mexico. A member of the American Institute of Architects and the American Academy in Rome, he has

2315

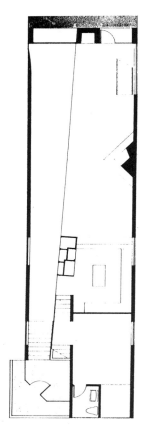

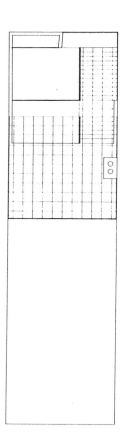

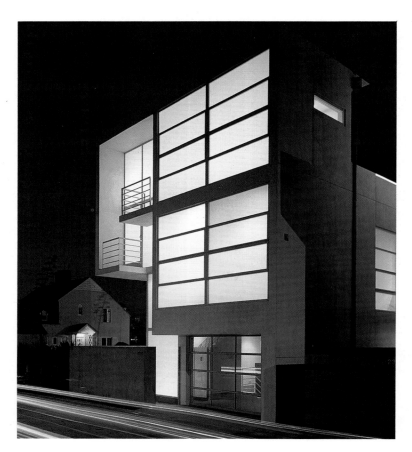

received a large number of awards and mentions. He is famous all over the world for his expositions and lectures, and has written many articles published in specialized magazines.

The house is built on three separate floors, on a rectangular base. A basement at ground level, partly hidden by concrete walls, is used for services and the garage. Access to the dwelling itself is at the rear, through a door located in one of the corners at the top of a few steps. The entrance leads into a large space containing no furniture, separation or feature which might interfere with the spatial continuity. Adjacent to this area, but separated, there is a spacious living room, dining room and kitchen. On the same floor but on a slightly different level there is also a study and bathroom. The stairway leading to the upper floor is at

Plans of the different levels.

Night-time view of the access facade at the rear of the building; entry is via a door in one of the corners.

On the ocean side, the concrete armatures resemble giant bleached bones along the shore.

one end of the living room. This floor is the night-time area, and it houses the master bedroom with *en suite* dressing room and private bathroom. The master bedroom opens onto a large, square terrace that projects the house towards the ocean. Two more bedrooms complete this floor. Tiled stairs lead up from the terrace to the upper roof terrace "bleachers" (a series of step-like benches which serve as a sun deck). This deck commands truly splendid view in all directions: the Pacific, the city lights by night, airplanes taking off from the Los Angeles airport, the town of Palos Verdes and Malibu beach.

One of the most distinctive features of this house is the use of materials and techniques which have a single common aim: to

A red steel pivot window frame pays homage to the colour of the Japanese flag.

Perspective of the stairway with wooden steps and metal banisters, connecting the different levels.

A granite runway inside the house introduces visitors to the aesthetic of Japan.

reflect the work itself in its shining floors and in the water, a basic element of the construction, so that the image produced is ever present, but always inverted.

On the ocean-side, the concrete armatures resemble gigantic bleached bones along the shore. A granite-clad retaining wall with water running over it is the only element which separates the house from a public walkway running along the beach six feet below. Here the black granite evokes the sedimentation of geological strata. The wet film on the granite forms a "water to water" visual bridge to the ocean when viewed from inside the house.

A red steel pivot window at the end of the axis pays homage to the color of the Japanese flag, just as the granite "runway" within the house propels the viewer towards Japan. The picture window, 9 feet wide and 13 feet high, pivots horizontally to cre-

ate a 13-foot-high opening with a view of the ocean. This important and very interesting viewpoint is flanked by a vertical cast-in-concrete glass slit which conducts light into the space, creating a kaleidoscope-like effect.

Inside the building, areas illuminated by the natural light diffused through obscure glass create lateral divisions and render a glowing dimensions to the end of the house which is accessible from the street. Upstairs, another concrete frame creates an

A film of water flowing over the granite wall adds water to water, establishing a visual bridge with the ocean when seen from the interior.

On the floors, cold dark ceramic and granite are combined with other areas covered with carpets made of natural materials.

aperture which frames the view of the ocean from the bed. The architect, Antoine Predock, chose materials that display a continuous and enriching contrast. The floors are covered with cold, dark ceramic and granite, and rugs made of natural materials. The external stairway leading to the roof deck is tiled, while the interior stairs combine wooden steps and metal banisters. Concrete and glass establish a constant dialogue. The red frame of the pivoted window competes with the white frames of the other openings and the interior stairway banisters, almost always in dark colors.

The prestigious architect Antoine Predock had absolutely no difficulty in connecting this single-family dwelling surrounded by other houses and clear signs of civilization with the savage, troubled waters of the Pacific Ocean, projecting it beyond the maritime walkway and the beach, spaces all too manipulated by man.

Interior of the functional kitchen with smooth pale walls.

View of the "runway", the fireplace area and the kitchen in the background.

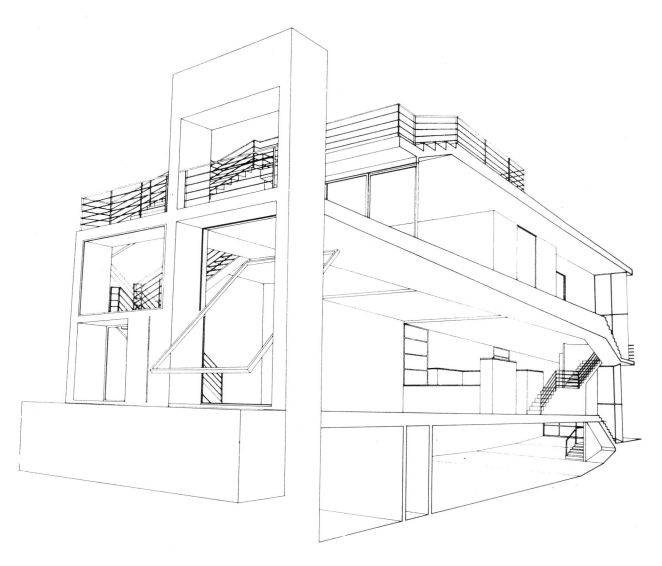

Exterior perspective of the house.

On the ocean side, the concrete armatures resemble giant bleached bones along the shore.

RITZ HOUSE

Vincent Mangeat

View of one of the volumes of the house.

Ritz House in planning this house Mangeat attempts a departure from the lyric, intimate concept which has governed his small-scale construction for so many years. This represents an investigation of dimensions through a spatial treatment that would be equally applicable to large constructions, but these smaller dimensions can be experienced more physically, more viscerally. Furthermore, the same magnificence and grandeur can be suggested on a domestic level is to demonstrate the repercussions that a building of any size and proportions may have on the setting, both conceptually and physically.

Mangeat believes that small residences offer an ideal area of experimentation, whose results may be applicable to larger constructions. Ritz House exemplifies the abstract notion of the reduced format, not in the conventional sense of a miniature but in the conversion of dimensions with no loss in expressive strength a small building can offer the same impressions as a larger one, but the observer can also experience other sensations that are closer, more intuitive.

Ritz House represents an attempt to realize these theories in practice without neglecting efficiency and functionality. It is located on steeply sloping land that is reached by an old road connecting the valley, upriver, with the town of Monthey. The steep, narrow road was the original local route for a farming

community. At the present time it connects numerous small residences scattered over the side of the side of the valley.

The building is sited on the steep gradient and is parallel to the road. The mountains is behind the house, which overlooks the scenic view of the valley. The execution of the construction not only affected the pre-existing topography; at the same time, the road was contoured to fulfil the new requirements of the house. The architect adheres to a standpoint that is all too frequently ignored: an intervention is not separate and independent of its physical context but must adapt itself to the existing fabric. This integration calls for an overall unifying planning process whether in the country or in the city.

The project consisted of two stages: the modernization and conditioning of the local road and the planning of the house in relation to its immediate context. These phases were considered by the architect to be simultaneous and complementary, representing one of the basic tenets of urban architecture: the limit between public and private space. Thus, the road was widened in some spots and its course was straightened. A large retaining wall was built to support the new structure. The hollow facing is executed in concrete and is characterized by niches that correspond with its structural units. This inner side of the wall encloses

Panoramic view of the house.

Section and axonometric plan of the house.

the terrain destined for the building of the residence. To offset the vertical tendency, its composition is longitudinal. The choice of reinforced concrete (both for the retaining wall of the widened sections of the road and for the base of the structure) is as effective as it is economical.

The organization, which is more imposed than suggested by this wall, involves the use of its hollow structures to accommodate washrooms and various facilities. This helps to define a static and compartmentalized space that reflects its practicality,

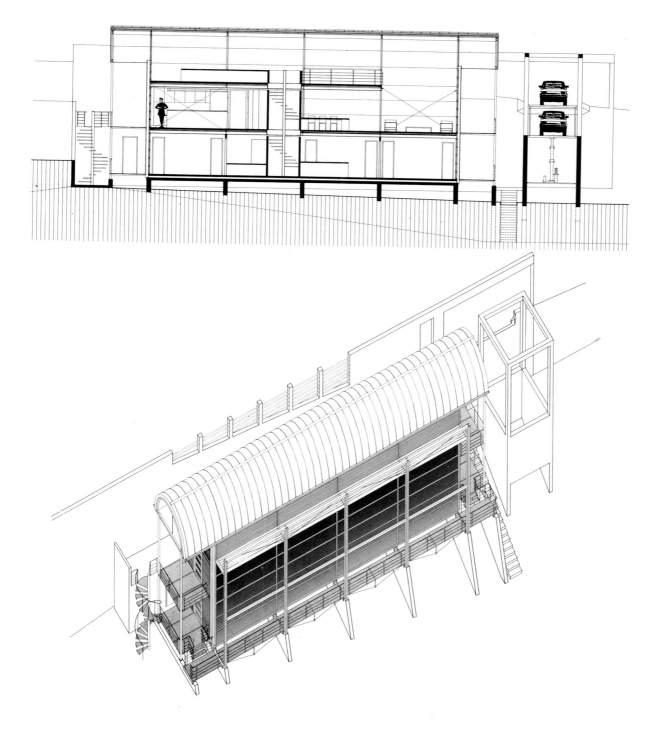

which is symbolized by the heaviness and rigidity of the wall. The two different stages of the project are thus connected in order to distribute the least significant areas according to their functional roles.

The rest of the house stands free of the retaining wall and is a parallel rectangular mass. This volume acquires a fluid, dynamic aspect that is related to the quality and rhythm of life represented in the living space. The impression is reinforced by the systematic use of metal, particularly in the zinc/titanium roof with its semi-cylindrical curve that lends movement to the exterior. The trapezoidal concrete structures that support the house grow progressively larger with the increasing gradient of the land.In this way a free-standing concrete base is formed from which the house rises. The pergola, also of metal, reaches the level of the roof, framing the vast visual perspective of the valley. This lends the house a sense of weightlessness that is very well suited to the spatial/functional relationship that the architect is attempting to suggest.

The volumetric configuration is dynamic free flowing and light. The metal finishes combine subtly with the nearly complete openness of the walls. Thermal glazing and insulating-lacquered aluminum door and window frames determine the exterior

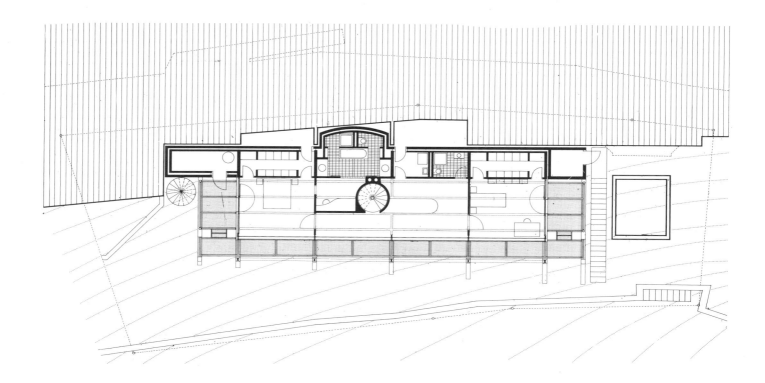

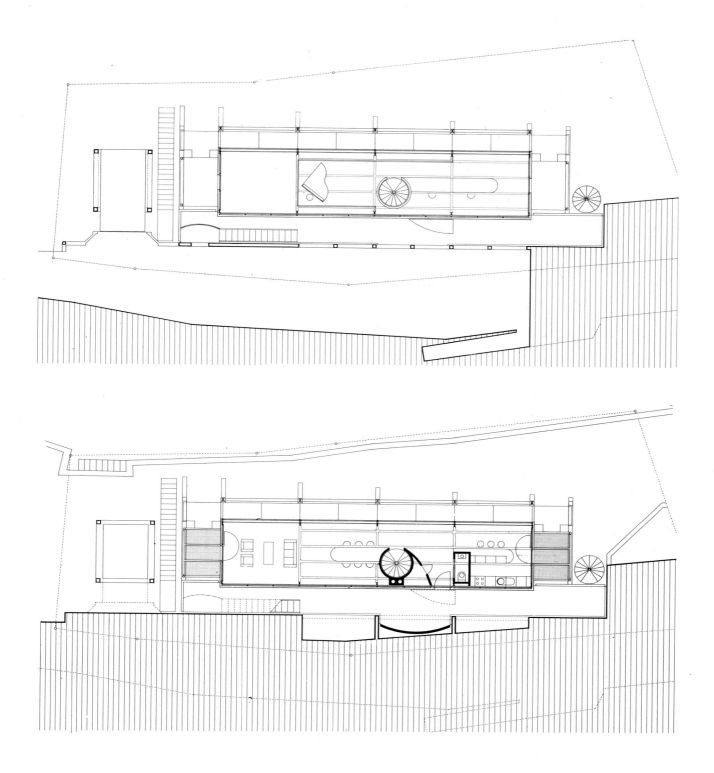

View of the main and first floors.

Plans of the main, first and second floors.

One of the accesses to the main floor.

appearance of the house. At both ends of the building the long semicylindrical body of the roof is extended to form small balconies on the floor levels. In this way, a relationship is maintained between the interior and the surrounding countryside. The external aspect of the residence is completed by communication elements such as the spiral staircase, the rectilinear flight of steps, that leads down to the lowest level of the terrain and the car elevator that communicates with the public roadway and serves as a garage. Between the free-standing base and the walls of the house there is an transitional area containing a lateral outdoor walkway protected by the pergola and a metal railing.

The relationship between the two construction stages (the improvement of the roadway) and the building of the structure itself) is established by the retaining wall. Mangeat distributed the functional programme in accord with the features imposed by the layout of the static, rigid wall. Thus, talking advantage of the situation of the recesses, he introduced the least important spaces (washrooms and facilities) in order to use the free-flowing, dynamic interior of the house for the major living areas. The transformation of the setting is to the public benefit, but it also contributes to the organization of a way of life that Mangeat attempts to define through his architecture.

The various interior areas are articulated on three levels. the bottom floor contains the bathrooms and the landry room, and two large bedrooms are situated at either end of the floor to benefit from the natural light from the exterior. The ground floor contains the kitchen, a smaller bathroom and a spacious living room/dining room. The position of the attic leaves space free for a double-height living room with a vertical perspective that culminates in the vaulted structure of the roof. In the attic is a large office whose ceiling is formed by the metal roof. The penetration of the exterior is achieved through the balconies formed by the extension of the semi-cylindrical body, supported on slender pillars and protected by plain railing. All of the components of these balconies are executed in aluminum.

There are two communication systems linking the three levels. Outside the spiral staircase connects the balconies of the ground and first floors. A flight of steps parallel to the retaining wall descends from the ground floor to the roadway. Inside the house is a cylindrical module of masonry that contains another spiral

Three different parts of the house: dinning room, bedroom and bathroom.

Interior of the top floor.

staircase. Its circular form is used to arrange several components of the built in furniture, such as the dining room table and the desk in the office, both of which are ash, with rectilinear forms terminating in curves.

In distributing the rooms, an attempt was made to maintain the longitudinal perspectives in so far as possible. The structural division is rather light, the only architectural obstacles being the central stairway cylinder and the partition walls of the bathrooms and installations. The distribution can be modified by rearranging the furniture, but a corridor along the glazed wall is always left free to preserve the visual perspective and the brightness and luminosity of all the rooms. The flooring, either in beech wood or tiles (as in the bathrooms with their unique patterns formed by bands of colour), the metal frames, the clean metal structures of the framework and the roof, as well as the use of continuous thermal glazing all contribute to the light, dynamic interior atmosphere appropriate to the life style that Mangeat attempts to express through the morphology employed.

This project by Vincent Mangeat represents a reflection on the theme of dimension and scale in architecture. His working concept is not that of miniaturization, but an attempt to provide the small residential format with a development that is a departure from the bucolic, intimate mood that is so frequently encountered in domestic architecture. The house is an experiment through which innovative impressions can be experienced more intensely than would be possible in a more monumental structure. The project influences both the physical and conceptual context, improving the transportation network and distributing the living space in response to exterior stimuli. The architect allocated the least significant functions to the recesses in the retaining wall, and the rest of the residence was given a longitudinal, free-flowing development. The interior treatment is perfectly suited to the way of life he attempts to define. In short, the project is an attempt to interpret the limits of proportion and scale, in spite of its reduced format, and approach the incommensurable.

Two details of the interior staircase.

Another view of the dinning/living room.

The children bedroom.

BERNASCONI HOUSE

Luigi Snozzi

Bernasconi House: view of the exterior.

Some of the constant themes defining the creative work of Luigi Snozzi are to be found in the construction of the Bernasconi House. Once again it is possible to observe an almost obsessive tendency towards the reduction and simplification of forms, a schematization which turns the volumes into components of a building considered as an object, the adaptation of the volumes to the topography, the need to make the interior areas match the surroundings in a suitable way and the thematic exploration of the entrances. It is through these aspects that this house must be understood. Geometric rigor, the desire to integrate, and the unmistakable naked appearance are revealed as the premises defining a personal style of understanding architecture.

The house is located in the Carona Valley, in an area characterized by a steep upward slope to the south, and a wide esplanade towards the northern flank. The attention the architect gives to the ground, and even to the subsoil, is revealed as one of the decisive characteristics of the emplacement. The morphology of the terrain itself provides the base of the project. Having understood the nature of the site, the distribution of the buildings is decided in advance, without any need to interfere with the surface. Due to this respect for nature the building is gently molded to the previous shape of the ground and fitted into the intersection of the slope and the flat surface at its base, thereby connecting the two zones. In this way a physical space is created which, despite formal differences, is unified by the arrangement of the volumes.

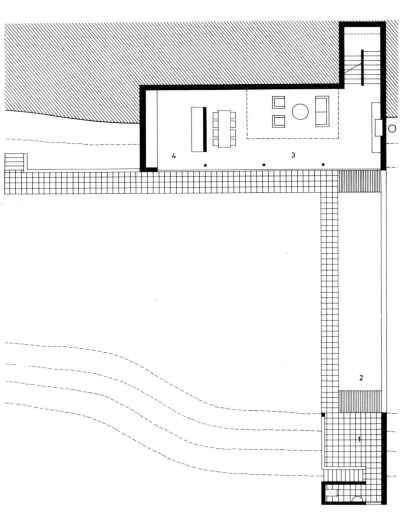

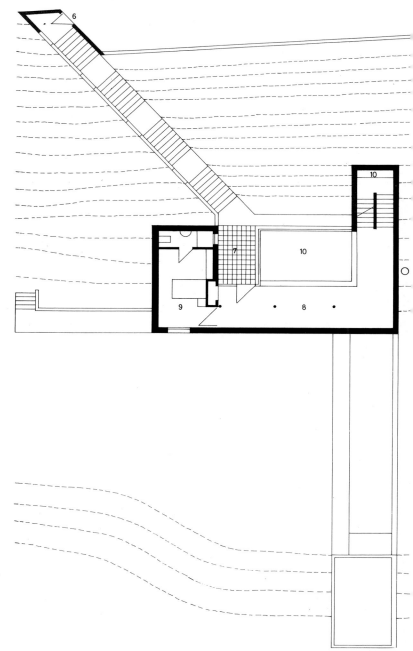

Plan of the main floor.

Plan of the first floor.

Plan of the top floor.

Plan of the second floor.

Night view of the house.

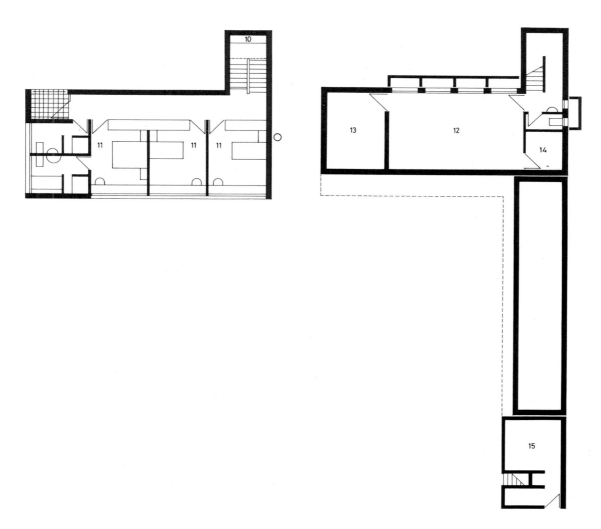

Access to the building is gained from an area at the highest level of the plot, which contains the parking space, and from which there is a view of the house from the south-west. A long flight of steps, laid out diagonally in order to cope with the unevenness of the terrain, descends from there. One then comes upon the opaque mass of the house, with its prolongation via the swimming pool and patio as far as the belvedere. Continuity and interdependence are established between the three elements of construction represented by the steps, the house, and the belvedere through a set of levels, directions, and orientations which confer a unique aesthetic effectiveness on the overall work.

The functional programe of the interior is that of a second home distributed over three floors, plus a basement containing a wine cellar. Above this is found the open-plan space containing the living-room/dining-room and the simple kitchen. This floor is situated on the same level as the swimming pool, and looks onto the valley. The next floor is where the grand flight of steps enters the small covered porch. Here we find the guest area, with a bedroom and toilet, and a study which reaches as far as the

Different views of the exterior of the house. The access to the building is from an area located in the highest part of the house.

Section of the house.

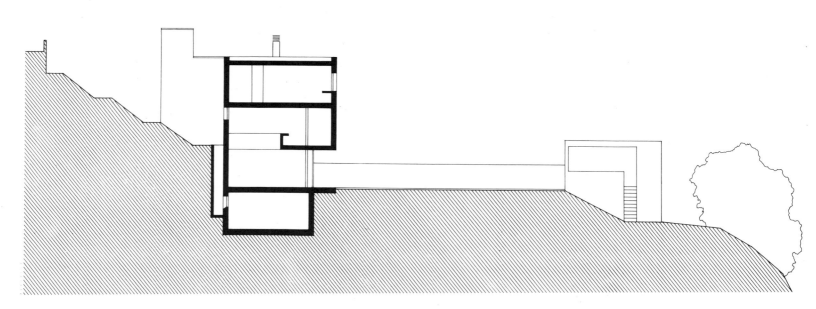

south-eastern sector where the stairs are situated. The stairs provide physical communication between the different levels of the house. The bedrooms and bathrooms are found on the top floor.

The simplicity of the interior programe is expressed in the facades in keeping with Snozzi's technical constants: bare concrete, simple volumes, and a strategic placing of windows and doors. The presence of two bodies may be perceived from the entrance: the first has a horizontal tendency and comprises the house itself; the second is vertical, rising above the main body, serves to communicate the various areas. The intersection of the ground and middle floors forms a covered hollow, a sort of portico, which provides entry to the interior. The continuation of the lower wall and a small strip of glass which rises to meet the opaque mass of the next floor complete the cold, hard aesthetics of the south-western facade. A small balcony at this eastern end is the only aperture looking out onto the mountain from the corridor on the floor containing the bedrooms.

The two side walls have little in the way of openings, although there is a narrow window on the eastern side of the upper floor. The most outstanding feature of the western side is the wall which originates in the belvedere, ascending in such a way as to match the shape of the slope, and runs alongside the swimming

pool offering quite a complicated structure. The living-room and kitchen communicate with the exterior by means of a fully-glazed wall which allows a play of reflections on the surface of the pool and provides a view of the valley framed by the belvedere. The two upper floors appear as a solid, compact mass, the opacity of which is only interrupted by a square window to one side of the middle floor and a rectangular one which provides the bedrooms with natural light. The volume projects slightly out over the lower floor in order to protect it from excessive sunlight. The windows are arranged in a calculated fashion in order to obtain the best relationship between the different rooms and the exterior, and also to obtain the best views of the landscape.

The treatment of the interior is also defined by the reduction and simplification of planes and elements. The floor on the same level as the swimming pool is open-plan, and appears as a unitary structure looking out onto the patio. A visual connection is created between the two lower floors by means of a rectangular opening in the ceiling of the living-room. This device enables an increase in the sense of space, light, and transparency on both floors and also provides the highest vertical perspective of the whole house apart from that of the stair tower. The impression of spaciousness is reinforced by the placing of a large fresco on the double interior wall formed by the opening leading to the first floor. The fresco is by Livio Bernasconi and it contributes towards emphasizing the quality of the interior. The solution of locating the stairs in a contiguous module also obeys these aims.

The lack of structural elements in the different rooms and the unadorned functional furniture are other elements contributing to the resolution of the interior. A few columns (three on the lower platform and two in the studio of the middle floor) are the only components not forming part of the superstructure, and they are used to aesthetic rather than functional ends. On the upper floor dividing walls are indispensable for separating the bedrooms. On the latter level the process of natural lighting is revealed as rather complex. The problem of lighting the rooms is resolved by the long window of the northern facade. Nevertheless, the real problem was posed by the need to light the interior corridor without disturbing the opaque mass facing the mountain. The solution was to open a gallery at one end of the external wall. Despite its smallness it provides a beautiful lighting effect which augments the visual quality of the interior space.

To the serene harmony of the contrast between the bare concrete and the glass is added the use of travertine marble both for the flooring and for the entrance steps. It is laid in 100 X 130cm slabs. Another of the creator's obsessions can be percei-

Another view of the swimming pool.

Two views of the living room located in the main floor.

Two views of one of the areas of the first floor.

ved in the nakedness of these elemental forms. Reduction is used not only as an instrument to aid understanding of the spatial order but also to create a dialogue between the building and the elements of the surrounding environment: such external agents as the sun, the wind, and the light form part of the fundamental concept of this work. This material is used in pursuit of a subtle modulation of the lighting effects on the steps and in the finish of the floors. The interiors are completed with double walls covered in light tones, plastered ceilings and varnished metalwork.

Luigi Snozzi's conception of architecture is clearly reflected in the construction of family houses in definitively natural settings. The house is perceived as a small element within the exis-

Aerial view showing the dining room and the first floor.

ting physical setting. This work is not presented as a formally resolved object situated in the terrain, but in fact adapts itself to it and attempts, with the greatest of respect, to embrace as much territory as possible. The location of the house is determined by the topography, and to initiate the project all that had to be done was to correctly interpret the environmental data. In this almost cosmic vision of artistry the house is presented devoid of ornament, with its simple volumes and structures practically uncovered in order to establish a sincere and stimulating dialogue with the external elements. The best definition of Snozzi's creative technique is to describe it as a tendency towards reduction and schematization as a means of subordination to the physical landscape and the environmental atmosphere.

The main bedroom located in the top floor.

OPPOSING VERTICAL AND HORIZONTAL PLANES

J. Frank Fitzgibbons

The horizontal lines of the northeast facade contrast with the south side in a play of opposites.

The counterpoising of the vertical and horizontal planes create a very contemporary architectural design.

The value of this project lies in J. Frank Fitzgibbons' intelligent use of a site with challenging natural topographical features. The resulting structure is tectonic in essence, and the architecture is defined by the peculiarities of the site.

The plot is relatively long, about 3.900 m^2 situated on top of a hill at the end of a private cul de sac. From this height, the house would afford spectacular views of the city of Los Angeles, and the Pacific Ocean beyond. But Fitzgibbons was faced with a topography which posed great difficulties: a very steep slope with irregular contours and a rugged terrain. The architect approached his task with a view to overcoming these drawbacks and turning them to advantage in the design of the residence. He sited the house on the highest pont of the steepest slope, near the street, thereby attaining several objectives: excellent panoramic views, a major reduction in construction costs, and the most economical use of the available land by extending the structure down the southern incline of the hill.

J. Frank Fitzgibbons completed his architectural training at the University of Michigan in 1966. For eleven years he was employed by various firms in New York, Berne and Rome. In 1977, he returned to the United States and settled permanently in Los Angeles. In 1985, he opened his own architecture and sculpture studio, where he took on commissions for commercial premises ,offices and restaurants, as well as for private houses. He has organized several exhibitions of his sculpture in Los Angeles, one of the most significant being a public show in the Pacific Design Center in 1988. He is a member of the American Institute of

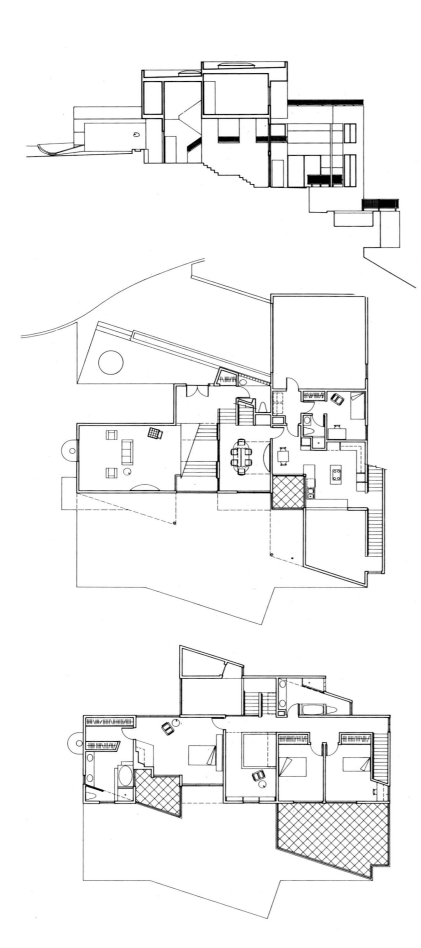

Architects, and president of the Architectural Foundation of Los Angeles. His projects have been published in *Toshu-Jukatu* (Japan, 1986), *LA Style* (USA, 1987-1988) and other professional magazines.

The main rectangular volume is arranged on a set of three terraces facing south, which facilitate the transition between the interior and the exterior, and attenuate the difference between the vertical plan of the building and the slope of the hill. The construction extends in two directions (one imposed by the topography and the other planned by the architect), thus achieving complete integration of the structural forms with the terrain. Fitzgibbons has created a magnificent harmony among the planes which constitute this southeast facade, through the interconnection and overlapping of the different floors, without forcing the design. In this project, the constructed masses and spaces have an individual tension and are balanced by their opposites within the composition.

Fitzgibbons also used another technique to handle the unevenness of the terrain. On the northwest facade, where the garage and main entrance are located, there are horizontal bands in different colors which reflect the interior changes in level. This was done to increase the visual importance of the base of the house, generating a sense of stability and allowing the structure to open to the exterior as much as possible, without provoking a sense of vertigo.

The house is constructed on three floors. The entrance level contains the living room, dining room and kitchen. The latter is connected to a family breakfast room, which in turn communicates with the maid's quarters and, the laundry room, via a stairway, with a family sitting room below, which gives direct access to the swimming pool. The main entrance divides this floor into two sections. The visitor may enter the dining room

South elevation

Plans of the different levels.

The south facade is open to the light and the countryside and descends in three terraces.

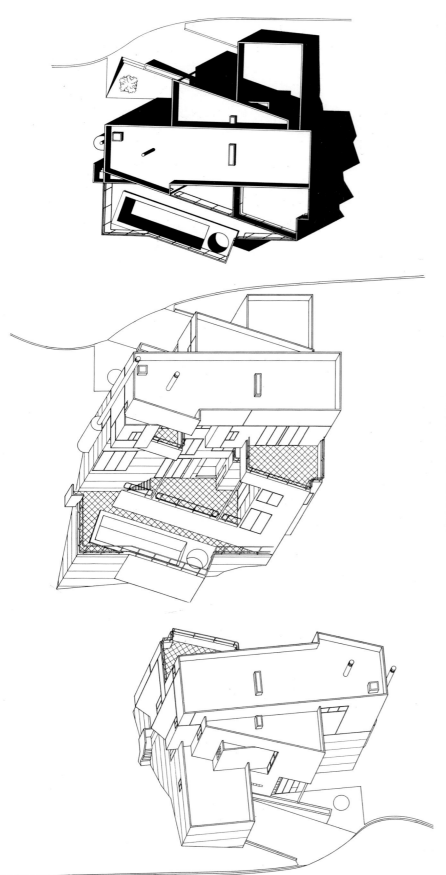

Plan view of the building.

Axonometric plans of the house from various angles.

The tunular chimney on the lateral wall is painted red, adding a touch of contrast.

and living room, or proceed straight ahead to the south end of the house, which offers a view of the swimming pool on the roof terrace overlooking Los Angeles. The lowest level accommodates the swimming pool, two sitting rooms, a dining room/terrace, a bar and a utility room. The areas which require peace and quiet, such as the bedrooms – each with its own balcony – and the library, are all on the top floor.

Inside, the partition walls do not reach the ceiling, designed by the architect as imperfect vertical planes. This technique creates an impression of open, spacious volumes pervaded by a cool, transparent atmosphere. The incomplete structuring of the partitions creates sight lines from the living room up to the first floor, and the stairway, which accentuates the feeling of free-flowing space. This double height living room structures the arrangement of the floors above and below it, and also acts as the communicating link with the exterior.

The terrace on the lowest level contains the light fiberglass swimming pool. This deck is supported by a beam which projects beyond the wall of this terrace. The inside or the swimming pool is painted a rust colour reminiscent of the earth and contrasting with the blue of the water.

Fitzgibbons has developed space and movement through

The steps invite the visitor to enter the house, which is open to the exterior.

Pillars, railings and the fence surrounding the property are all painted mauve to contrast with the exterior walls.

vertical and horizontal planes to create a contemporary architectural and interior design. The sense of peace and harmony in the individual spaces fuses with movement and the resulting dynamic is soothing.

The entire house is enlivened by the interaction of Yin and Yang forces, which influence both the architecture and the interior design. Fitzgibbons has orchestrated the concepts of interior and exterior, as well as the temporal notions of past, present and future to create this significant contribution to the art of architecture.

The long narrow pool is balanced by the adjacent small round one. The two pools seen from the terrace of the second floor.

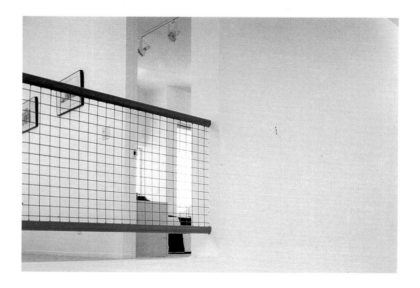

The colour motifs from outside the house are also repeated inside. The colour scheme softens the separation between the different levels.

*The glass dining room table rests on two undulating metal supports. The
city of Los Angeles can be seen through the window.*

The open spacious feeling of the rooms is enhanced by the walls stopping short of the ceiling. The wooden floor adds warmth to the living room.

Corner of the living area; the bronze sculpture of the human form sems to contemplate the countryside.

The staircase leading to the first floor. The entrance to the living room is on the left, picked out by the red finish on the inside of the arch.

The wooden staircase leading up to the dining room.

The chimney seen from behind the banisters. The chimney stack attached to the external wall is painted red.

LANDSCAPE IN THE LEADING ROLE

Jerónimo Junquera y Estanislao Pérez Pita

The volumetrics of the house are neat and simple, with a square ground plan broken up into smaller squares.

Within one breathtaking landscape these two architects, Jerónimo Junquera and Estanislao Pérez Pita, have been able to transform and integrate the surroundings into their design. This single-family dwelling rises up in aesthetic defiance of the Bay of Biscay, projecting its aura of intimacy into the far-off horizon.

The house is situated on a ridge overlooking the bay of Santander, Spain, over the Cubas estuary, with the town of Santander itself as a backdrop. From climatic point of view, this location defies the construction conditions of the area, since the blustery north winds and the heavy western rains are primary factors to be taken into consideration with regard to choice of site. Facing this challenge, however, the area offers an incomparably picturesque landscape which spreads out like a fan from north to west and finally south, covering the Bay of Biscay the bay and town of Santander, the Picos de Europa mountain range and the Cubas estuary. The terrain of smooth hills is surrounded by numerous single-family constructions. In spite of the profusion of these rural dwellings, the overall setting is peaceful and creates the sensation of order and balance.

Jerónimo Junquera was born in Madrid in 1943. He studied architecture at Madrid's Escuela Técnica Superior and graduated in 1969. since 1973 he has been working in partnership with Estanislao Pérez Pita, and both architects shared the editorship of the magazine *Arquitectura* from 1977 to 1980. In 1986 he chaired a seminar on land-sea limitations in the Universidad Internacional Menéndez Pelayo in Santander.

Estanislao Pérez Pita was also born in Madrid in 1943. He grad-

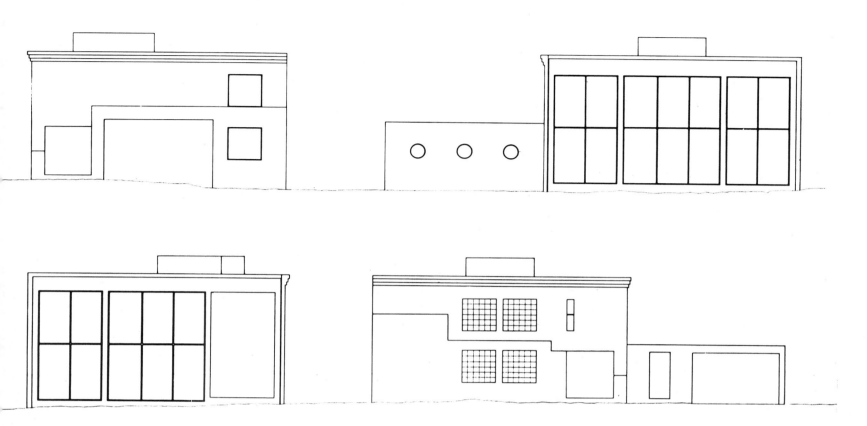

uated in Architecture in 1969 from the Escuela Técnica Superior in Madrid. In 1968 and 1969 he worked with José Antonio Corrales, and in 1970 and 1971 in New York with Davies, Brody and Associates. He has been lecturer in charge of "Projects II" (1971) and of the end of course project (1976) at Madrid's Escuela de Arquitectura. He delivered a seminar on restoration at the Universidad Internacional Menéndez Pelayo in Cuenca (Spain, 1985) and from 1986 to 1990 he worked as associate lecturer on the "Projects III" course at Madrid's Escuela de Arquitectura.

The numerous specialist magazines in which their work has been published, the articles they have written in the press, the countless lectures delivered by them all over Spain, New Zealand and in Sydney, their contributions to conferences and seminars, the exhibitions of their work and the prizes and honors they have received are a sure guarantee of the quality of their many achievements.

This house is laid out in the shape of a cube closed off to the north and east and open, in contrast, to the south and west, inside which there is another smaller cube housing the living area, surrounded by a large space leading to the housing the living area, surrounded by a large space leading to the outside area, which consists of a conservatory forming a kind of internal garden. The diagonal line generates a circular sequence; on top of this primary structure lie several superimposed terraces whose

Detail of the facade. Large windows which give the observer a view of the interior.

North elevation.

West elevation.

South elevation.

East elevation.

geometry is totally different and which soften the radical nature of the angular geometry.

In this house, divided onto two levels, shared units have been separated from private areas. The lower level has been used for the lounges, the dining room and kitchen. The upper level, to which one gains access via a staircase decorated with plants, houses the bedroom which opens directly onto the staircase, porch and two bathrooms.

The aim of this project is to provide an answer to a series of objectives worked out from an analysis of reactions to the environment, reactions towards which rural dwellings have been moving over the years, not forgetting the shape they take within their surroundings. The creators of this holiday dwelling, which is atypical within its own particular context, opted for a structure which would respect the symmetrical arrangement, i.e. the building is constructed in accordance with the north-south and

Angle of the facade. The interior is arranged on two levels, each containing spacious open areas

east-west axes. The volumetrics chosen are also clear and simple, represented by a square ground plan subdivided into smaller squares, and a volume formed by the addition for cubes; to this volume the architects have added all the different utility areas, with a notable emphasis on the protection of living spaces. In this case the problem is not only rain, but also wind, and thus to link the outside with the inside the solution of a glass porch was adopted. This porch faces south and west, the intention being to obtain a greenhouse effect. In this way a glass cube makes up the external structure, and the house inside this cube transforms it into an amazing bay window; the transparency of the walls establishes intelligent dialogue between outside and inside, and the bright Biscay sunlight is drawn in to every corner of the dwelling. The ivy and creepers growing inside the house help to extend the decoration towards the horizon and also make the green hues of the plants more intense.

The house loses transparency and closes up to the outside on the north elevation.

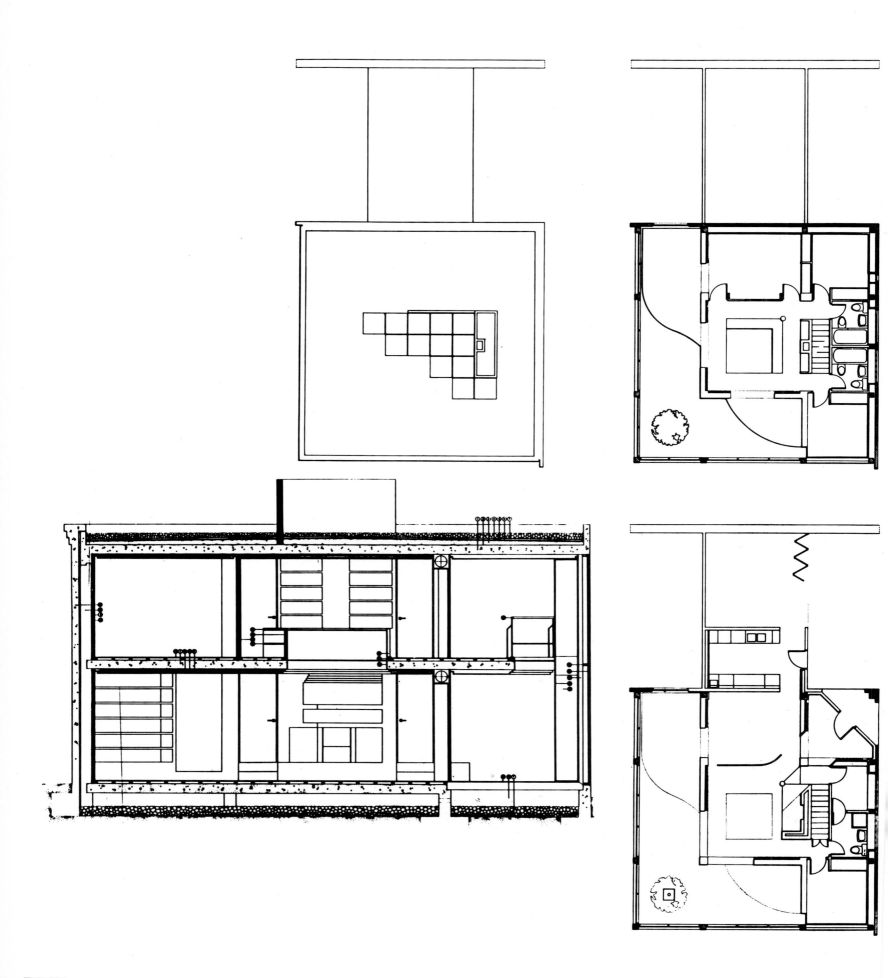

All floors in the house are of varnished wood raised in plat-forms, and the walls have all been painted white so as to reflect light and so that the observer's attention is not distracted from the real protagonist of this domestic stage – the landscape. As regards interior decoration, the architects have continued to highlight the natural environment outside the structure. The furni-ture inside the house is sparse but well chosen and, of course, directs one's gaze outside. In the lounge, a large leather sofa and a few simple wooden easy chairs with black and white striped canvas backrests and seats constitute the rest and relax-ation area, dominated by a table. A fireplace sunk into a wall and some shelving complete this part of the house.

The dining room opposite the large windows is comprised of a simple iron table and ordinary wooden chairs with bulrush seats. In the bedroom the decor is equally sparse, and a few mattresses covered with more striped canvas are sufficient to create the ideal place for slumber. The floor is tiled in cork. In the

Plan of the lower level.

Cross section of the dwelling.

Upper floor.

Ground floor.

View of the south facade. To the left, the table on the porch, and two easy chairs to the right.

bathroom a two-piece glass block wall has been constructed – these two parts open out for ventilation purposes. White has been chosen as the color for the toilets, and the same platform effect is to be found on the floor. The staircase railing consists of painted metallic tubes designed by Manolo Gallego. The wood-work is all Astrowall aluminium with neoprene joints.

This dwelling constructed by Jerónimo Junquera and Estanislao Pérez Pita brings the magnificent surrounding scenery into the house and transforms it into the most important feature of the decor. In this way the architects get the best out of the building's privileged location, a building which blends spontaneously into its surroundings thanks to the transparency of the glass, with no discrepancy between inside and outside. The end result allows immediate scenery to extend outwards and the far-off scenery to become a part of the intimacy of a private dwelling.

The plants intensify the vivid green surroundings.

Angle of the elevation. Two simple reclining wood and canvas chairs in a corner forest and relaxation.

The slightly rustic kitchen is a mixture of wood and white paint.

The dining-room is oposite the large windows. It consists of an extremly simple iron table and wooden chairs with bulrusch seats.

View of the porch. The staircase to the upper floor with banister fashioned from painted metal tubing designed by Manolo Gallego.

Detail of the bathroom. Adjustable parts on the window for the purposes of ventilation.

ARCHITECTURE OPEN TO ITS SURROUNDINGS

Mark Mack, de Batey & Mack

The basically rectangular shape of the construction is broken only by the patios and small windows in the thick concrete wall.

The Kirlin House lies in the middle of a 25 acre vineyard plot, and is a passive solar house designed to use sunlight to maximum advantage: the overhanging roofs permit the winter but not the summer sun to enter.

This completely flat site is located in Napa Valley, California, and is surrounded by vegetation and hanging vines, typical of the area. Its concealed position on a large clearing is most favorable, and it rises up defiant and mysterious from behind the wall.

The dwelling was designed by Mark Mack, de Batey & Mack, a company based in San Francisco, USA. He was born in Judenburg, Austria in 1949. Initially he studied at the Technische Hochschule in Graz, and subsequently at Vienna's Fine Arts Academy. During this period he worked for Steiger & Partners in Zurich, and for Hans Hollein in Vienna. He graduated in 1973, moved to New York and later to the area around the San Francisco bay, where he set up his own practice. In 1978 he went into partnership with Andrew Batey and founded *Archetype Magazine*. In this magazine he wrote that, during his association with Batey, the pair had a kind of gentlemen's agreement relating to the search for expressive and formal approaches to their work. In 1984 he set up his own architecture practice. He has been a guest lecturer at several academic establishments in Europe and the United States, he has also lectured at some of the most prestigious American universities and since 1986 has held the post of Associate Professor of Architecture at the University of California Los Angeles.

The aim of Batey & Mack's design was to comply as far as possible with the wishes of the client within a range of basic plan types such as rectangle, a square or a cross, putting these together in L-shapes, U-shapes, H-shapes, etc. This approach is extremely flexible for the expression of a wide range of idiosyncrasies.

This construction is arranged around two courtyards with different orientations: the south courtyard is an exterior winter living area, while in the north courtyard the architect built a fresh and shady summer area. A striking feature of the main facade is the wall, which is divided into two sections and closes protectively around the dwelling. It does in fact protect the dwelling like a medieval fortress, and seeks to protect its intimate corners. The center of this wall is occupied by a square entrance topped by a wooden roof which gives access to the courtyard. This area is floored in ochre tiles, and contains a blue edge structure which leads directly to the wooden entrance door.

The construction is basically rectangular in shape, and this format is broken only by the patios and openings on the thick concrete wall which heightens the closed and centripetal appearance of the structure. This area constitutes the access zone, and has been designed as a summer living space where water dribbles down a stone shaft, carved by Larry Shank, into a small pool.

The south facade was executed entirely in glass. The overhang of the roof is calculated to allow the interior of the dwelling

Detail of the south facade seen from the vineyard. The importance of the wall is shown by the slope of the roof with reference to its upper line.

View of the south facade of the house. The thick wall is stepped on either side and contrasts sharply with the metal roof with skylight windows.

Gravel covered courtyard on the south side. All the walls are glass and the overhanging eaves permit the winter but not the summer sun to enter.

to be heated during the winter months, since at this time of year the sun lies low in the sky. The courtyard is gravelled, and thus constitutes a formal response producing a surface pleasing to the eye. Access to this part of the dwelling is via a stairway, executed in the same material as the rest of the house. The importance of the wall is shown by the slope of the roof with reference to its upper line.

Access to the property is through the wooden door on the northern elevation, set into the wall itself. Without breaking the unity and continuity of the entire structure, the interior follows the same simple format as the exterior, the most obvious example being the use of the same flooring material as on the courtyard. A concrete block mass closes off this area, separating it from other zones without however interrupting the spatial continuity of

Drawing of the north facade and plan of the house.

Detail of the steps which lead down to the rear gravelled patio.

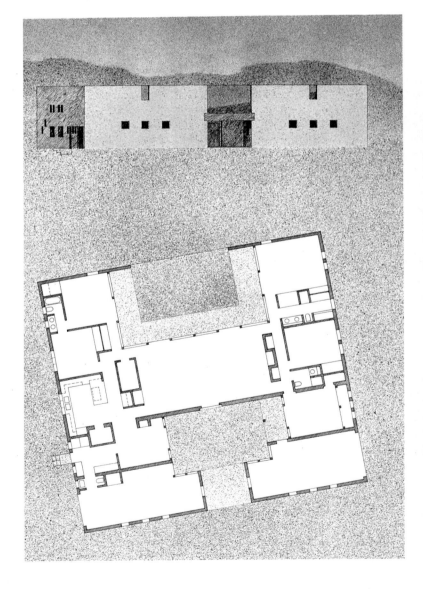

View of the inner courtyard and the front door of the house seen through the wooden roofed entrance.

Detail of the south facade.

the wooden ceiling, which can be seen from the inside and forms part of the definition.

The concrete block masses function as heat-collectors; the fireplace and the wine store are used for thermal storage. There is an electrical floor heating system throughout the interior but the owners rarely use it, given the favorable orientation of the dwelling.

The family area containing the fireplace is a most original room, since it is enclosed by a small stone wall which does not stretch the full distance to the ceiling. Thus it creates the effect of spaciousness, an effect enhanced by the white wooden ceiling. It contains few pieces of furniture and the large glass wall provides a view of the vineyards. The architects were responsible for the design of most of the furniture, and all the pieces are extremely simple. The materials used are also simple and represent a continuation of the exterior. A number of sky-lights let in sunlight to brighten the room.

The kitchen, concealed by one of the concrete blocks, is an essentially functional space. The same flooring as in the other rooms and a wooden roof give it a warm, cosy atmosphere. A kitchen counter has been built in an adjacent space for quick snacks.

The discreet elegance of the living room/dining room opens up completely to the patio on the southern slope of the dwelling through the all glass area, and this creates brightness and pleasant temperatures in winter. This room is extremely spacious, and the furniture in the rest and relaxation area and the dining area is all wooden. Behind the dining room table there is another stone wall, with seats made from the same material. The ceiling is wooden and the room is floored with ochre tiles. The bedrooms and bathrooms follow the same decorative lines, as does the cellar.

Thus the structural programe of the Kirlin Residence built by Mark Mack in Napa Valley is directed towards the interior of the

A striking feature of the main facade is the high wall, divided into two sectors, which closes protectively around the dwelling.

Entrance to the inner patio with concrete walls and wooden roof.

The front door.

dwelling. The protective wall encloses the structure and shields it from exterior threat. The structure is placed so as to take advantage of the most favorable temperatures all year round. There are two patios -the summer patio facing north and the south-facing patio which captures the winter but not the summer sun because of the overhang of the roof, built at an angle calculated to achieve this effect. This whole arrangement is reinforced by a backup heating system based on electrical wires in the baseboard. The interior follows a programe arranged around two large concrete blocks which form the internal boundaries. All these features follow a simple and sober arrangement which culminates in a pure residential unit, broken only by the patios and the small number of openings on the thick walls, turning the architecture towards the interior of the building.

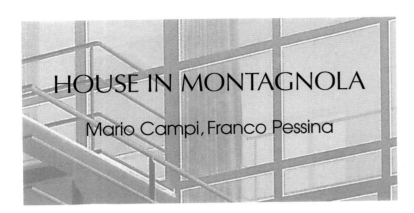

HOUSE IN MONTAGNOLA

Mario Campi, Franco Pessina

The residence built by the Swiss architects Mario Campi and Franco Pessina on the slope of Montagnola Hill reaffirms the expressive coherence of this partnership. The simplicity of the plan, so close to the precepts of the Mediterranean structural rationalism, is based on a precise reading of the spatial characteristics, the most economical use of the topographical formation and a volumetric design that initiates an interesting dialogue between the architecture and its excellent position in the surrounding countryside. The two have created a structure that is distinguished by its geometric precision, expressive power and unifying concept. In addition to these architectural qualities, the tripartite functional programe introduced is governed chiefly by the relationship between interior and exterior spaces, based on the notions of transparency and luminosity. The economy of the composition and the use of a homogeneous vocabulary are consistent elements in Campi and Pessina's work.

These three terraced units are situated on a steep slope of Montagnola Hill in the city of Lugano. The architectural setting, dominated by conventional houses, serves to establish a plastic contrast among the various building styles. The site is rather inconvenient due to its long, narrow shape and abrupt incline. The terrain is developed from west to east, starting from the highest contour elevation, at the level of Via Matorell. This exceptional position affords magnificent views of the valley, the city and the splendid lake to the west. The layout of the house represents an attempt to initiate communication with both the immediate landscape and the larger visual scale.

Side view of the house.

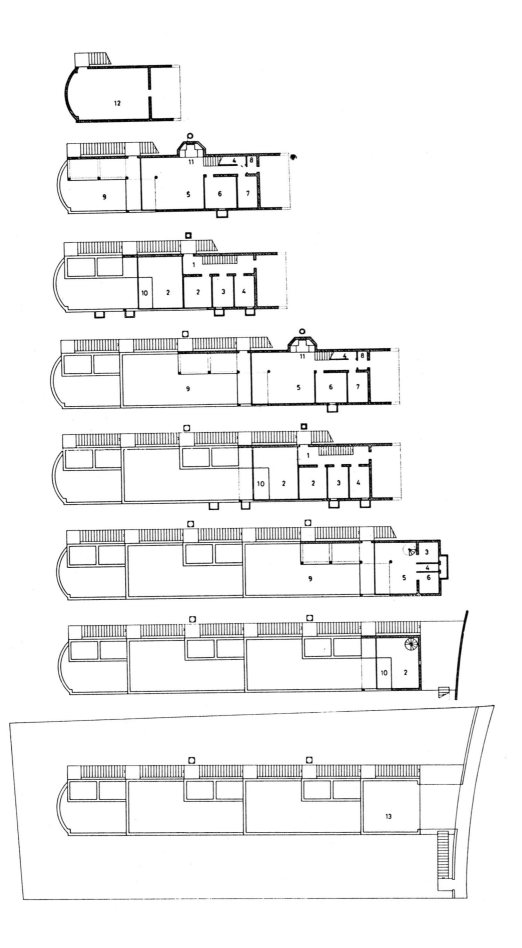

Plans showing the different levels of the houses.

Views of the two sides of the building.

In this difficult but imposing setting, the architects decided not to divide the three modules. They form one unified block molded with extreme naturalness to the topographical contours, the levels descending the entire length of the slope and adopting a progressive modular design. The basic source was a prior reading of the terrain that pursued as primary goals a lucid organization of the programe (both visually and functionally), an accentuated structural rhythm and a satisfying interaction between the architecture and nature.

The project thus consisted of the linear development of a unified mass, descending from west to east, expressed as three attached superimposed modules that define a natural continuity with the immediate and more distant landscape. From the outside the complex seems to be one unit, but its regular, simple geometry forms three articulated components in which the same visual scheme is reproduced. Apart from the impression of simplicity and transparency. Campi and Pessina's language is not an elementary code. On the contrary, the richness of their work is generally based on the fact that, with an expressive economy of means, they succeed in creating a network of extremely complex interconnections.

From this standpoint, the architect style is rather distant from the expressionist rationalism of Le Corbusier and closer to the

Two sections of both sides.

indigenous Mediterranean movement exemplified in Italy by the Figini and Pollini School, by Libera and particularly by Giuseppe Terragni. Their affinity is evidenced by the geometrical precision and structural logic that dominate the building, imposing a natural functional distribution and demarcating the facades and volumes. With these components the architects use a vocabulary that is pure rather than elementary, with connections in all directions and on all planes, between presence and absence, space and mass, achieving an aesthetic balance and a notable conceptual elegance.

The Montagnola houses reflect these rationalist principles in the strategic articulation of the masses, in the highly coherent geometric progression and in the impressive brightness and luminosity of the interior. The layout of the various structural elements forms a volume that cascades downward from the highest level, at the Via Matorell, and its external appearance is determined by the various ways in which this extreme difference in levels is handled. The flight of steps that provides access to the three units is built against the south facade. Its aspect is more closed

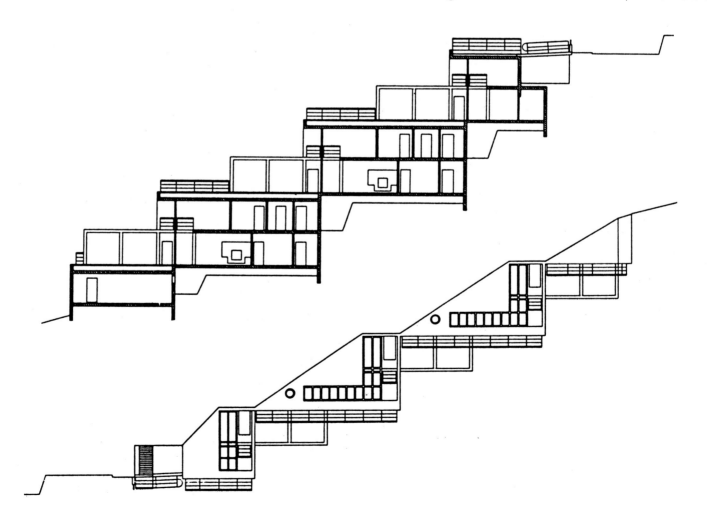

and compact, revealing the levels of the six surfaces, which are interpreted in the interior as duplexes and double heights. There is a door to each unit on every other level. The opposite elevation is more open and does not conceal the slope of the hill, calling attention to the adaptation of the structure to the terrain. The basic geometry of the building is articulated on the northern slope in the three volumes of the housing units.

From a frontal perspective, the complex also reflects the themes of progression and symmetry. Rising from the lowest curved surface of the cellar, the construction ascends the slope, with a terrace and a glazed facade that is repeated three times. The result is an interplay of the static and the dynamic, the opaque and the transparent and the exposed concrete and the glazing. The forms are pure and rigid in their highly simple volumetric configuration and their serene arrangement on the hill. In contrast, the overall complex appears free-flowing and mobile, owing to the themes introduced in its layout: depth, luminosity and hierarchy.

At this point it is worth mentioning the complex visual relationships that Campi and Pessina have successfully integrated in the residence by means of basic and elementary forms. Firstly, the pergolas on the west face provide tension and at the same time a certain visual ordering. These structures are formed at the meeting of the extension of the west face provide tension and at the same time a certain visual ordering. The partitions that protect the privacy of these terrace areas are reflected in the overall design by the formal difference between each of the lateral facades. This distinction is reinforced by the precise placement of openings in the elevations, which particularly affects the visual rhythm of the composition. These openings interrupt the simple, symmetrical scheme and, without sacrificing the aesthetic balance, they introduce new elements in the spatial relationship.

To distribute the programe properly, the architects designed an interior layout in which the more significant rooms communicate with the best views of the setting, in so far as this was possi-

The entrances of the different houses.

A nice view over Lugano's lake.

ble. In pursuit of this goal, Campi and Pessina centered their work on the motifs of space and light, ordering the different rooms according to the scenery. The three modules were laid out in the same way, although the highest of them is smaller.

The two end components contain communal facilities. On the top level, that of the Via Matorell, is a parking area. The cellar on the bottom level is curvilinear and is integrated naturally with the terrain. Each volume has two floors and an entrance on the south flank that is reached by the descending flight of steps built against that wall. The complex has a total of seven horizontal planes, which have a greater vertical development on the living-room levels, achieved through an opening in the slab that separates the floors, thus creating the double height. The more important rooms (the living room/dining room and the master bedroom) are in this area, communicating with the exterior through a continuous glazing that begins on the northern front. In addition to the entrance halls and the vast living rooms, the ground floor also houses the kitchen, bathrooms and other facilities. These latter spaces are partially underground because of the gradient of the land. The fireplaces are on the south, penetrating the terrain. To solve the problem of the smoke outlet, the flues emerge from the ground at a point beyond the lateral flight of steps, creating a striking visual effect. On the second level, the rooms overlooking the valley open onto small balconies whose supporting structures in reinforced cement are extended to form the pergolas that frame the visual sequences from the interior rooms. To make the most of the available space, the roof of each module serves as the terrace for the one above it, one of

The stairs leading to the entrances.

One of the terraces.

View of the living room that also shows the two levels of the house.

the most effective strategies of the complex. Their light metal railings and the grass growing on the outer section create a visual transition to the greenery of the landscape.

Mario Campi and Franco Pessina's design for this small residential building is based on the precepts of Mediterranean rationalism. Using a pure, limited geometric vocabulary, they succeed in establishing a highly complex network of relationships. All of the elements pursue a formal and conceptual link between the architecture and the setting through the adaptation to the topography, the progressive ordering of the masses, their visual rhythm, the alternation of transparency and opacity and the disparate treatment of the elevations. Although the components are basically static, they take on a dynamic and free-flowing appearance, elegantly expressing the construction process with its interior programe.

Access to one of the houses from the terrace.

View of the terrace from the inside.

The dining-room with direct access to the kitchen.

The main bedroom in the upper level.

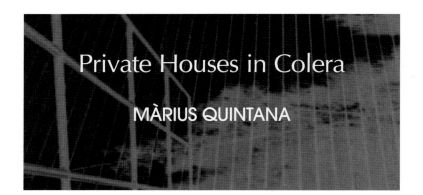

Private Houses in Colera

MÀRIUS QUINTANA

The house is structured by three wooden platforms.

The building stands in a striking position on the sea front, on land classed as Garden City 2, but affected by the Spanish Ministry of Public Works and the Environment's Coasts Act.

The project pertains to a preexisting building of little architectural value, used as a residence. The aim was to produce a functional, characteristic plan for a six-person holiday home.

Respect for the site and preexisting construction was mandatory, since the house and the land were both partially affected by the Coasts Act, as mentioned above. It was for this reason that architect Màrius Quintana proposed habitability improvements and structural repairs necessitating new building work on loadbearing walls, frames and facades.

The building is based on a structure with loadbearing walls in brick with metal pillars, with flat concrete summers forming horizontal porticoes. The facades are in brick with a five-cm air chamber filled with expanded polyvinyl chloride, with an additional inner wall of hollow brick. All the facing is in Portland cement mortar, smooth on the exterior and somewhat rougher on the interior, with visible swirls on walls and ceilings. The ceiling features are set at right angles, without mouldings. White is a constant throughout the project: the surfaces are finely plastered in powdered marble, with a smooth finish on the walls and ceilings. The metalwork on the railings is treated and painted in black enamel.

The lintels on the windows and sliding glass doors are in prefabricated ceramic and provide a minimum span of 20 cm.

All the roof surfaces are flat, with concrete slabs forming

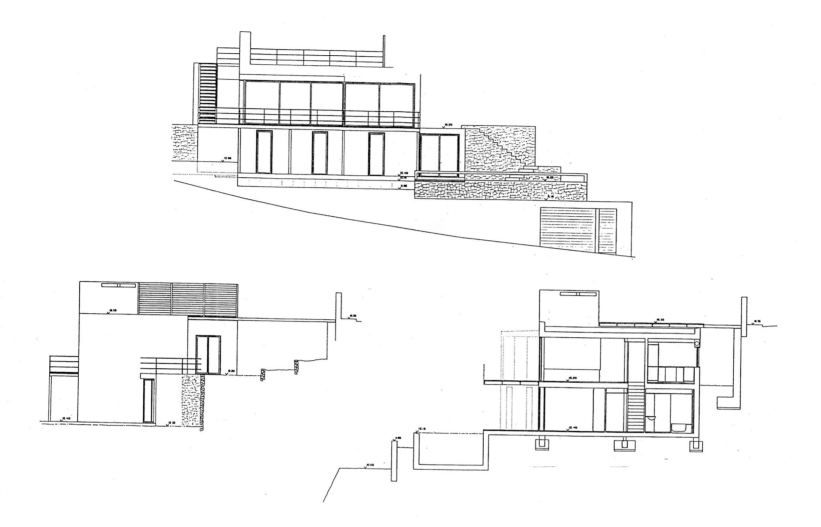

The terrace has a wooden floor.

Plan and section of the buildings.

slopes of at least 2%. On top of this there is a double layer of hollow bricks, treated with polyester asphalt sheeting to ensure impermeability. This in turn is partially covered with metal beams with a supporting lattice of wood, steam-treated with copper salts, the remainder being protected by a geotextile fabric covered with a layer of at least 15 cm of river gravel.

The terrace adjoining the ground-floor bedrooms is built on a concrete base. On the upper part, the layer of gravel is bricked over with blocks of travertine that form a slope leading to the garden.

The galvanized metal frames are built into the masonry of the house, and feature white lacquered aluminium fittings. The openings are double glazed and of various types: sliding, hinged, etc. The interiors of the frames are fitted in Flemish wood. The doors are featureless on both sides, with locks recessed into the edge and aluminium latches.

View of the external part of the dwelling.

The roof garden.

Two plans of the roof.

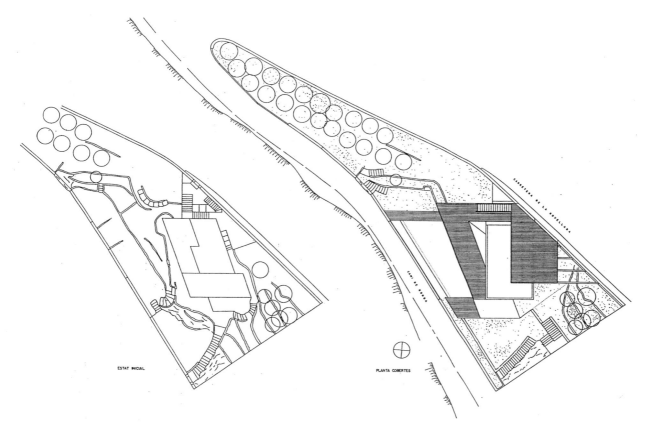

ESTAT INICIAL

PLANTA COBERTES

183

Màrius Quintana was born in Barcelona in 1954. He graduated in Architecture from the School of Architecture of Barcelona (ETSAB) in 1979, since then he has held several positions in the architectural profession in Barcelona City Council and, from 1982 to 1992, in the firm Santa & Cole. His teaching career began in 1989 in the Elisava Design School in Barcelona, and from that year to the present day he has taught at the School of Architecture of the Vallès. He also took part in the conference of Young European Architects *La Città e il ¿Plume?*, in Italy in 1986. He has built a considerable number of architectural projects, which have earned him several awards. Some of the most outstanding of Màrius Quintana's prizewinning works are: Joan Miró Square in Barcelona, Villette Park in Paris, Santa Ana Square in Mataró (Barcelona province), the remodelling of Rambla Catalunya in Barcelona, the exhibition *Eina, 20 anys d'Avantguarda*, the design "Lamparaalla", winner of the ADIFAD Silver Delta Prize, and his design for the restricted entry competition *Stan aan de Stroom* organized by Antwerp City Council. He was also short-listed for the II Biennial of Spanish Architecture in 1991-2 for his remodelling of Barcelona's Cathedral Avenue.

The improvements to the house we are concerned with here have succeeded in rationalizing the distribution so as to command better views of the sea, also adding to the preexisting volume two wooden platforms which enhance the building's relationship with the site and provide extra living space.

The higher of the two new platforms is on street level. It has a metal structure and wooden flooring, and forms a deck connecting the house to the street. It functions as a car parking area and the main entrance to the house. The metal structure of the

Views of different parts of the house: swimming pool, terrace and main facade.

platform is independent of the house itself and consists of girders on pillars and support beams, on top of which is laid the flooring, in wood steam-treated with copper salts.

The first-floor platform relates the living room to the upper garden, which extends to the end of the property. The two platforms communicate on the western side of the house via a metal staircase with gold-laminated fittings. The weld joints were polished to eliminate cavities which could cause rust. The steps are in wood.

The shape of the first floor is irregular due to the original perimeter being preserved intact. This is the area which contains the more communal living space: in the interior, the dining-living room and the staircase leading to the ground floor, and on the exterior, the terrace. The nucleus formed by the staircase together with the kitchen and bathrooms establish a new axis, different from that existing prior to the improvements, as it relates to the new structural elements and circulation routes. The chimney, the only structure that protrudes from the roof, also follows this new axis.

A third platform, built on ground level, connects the bedrooms to the lower garden and the swimming pool. The layout of these rooms is irregular in order to adapt them to the topography

The garden furniture on the main terrace.

View of the living room.

The main floor and first floor.

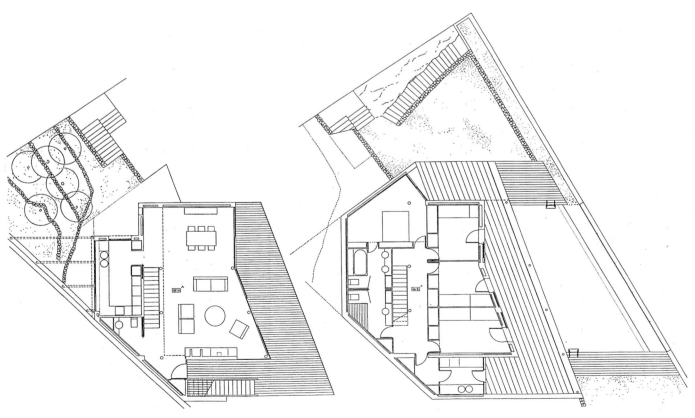

The main of the first floor offers the largest perspective of the interior.

Detail of the glass staircase.

and obtain the best possible views of the sea. The pool marks the edge of the property, where it meets the coastal footpath leading to the beach.

An overflow was built along the length of the swimming pool, alongside the coastal path, and in the section of garden between the house and the path there is a semisunken service shed which houses the regulator tank for the overspill from the pool and the filtering equipment.

This alignment is determined by the posts marking the boundary between the inland and coastal zones. Both the shed and the swimming pool stand free from the boundary wall of the property, and the whole design of the project thus leaves the public thoroughfare unaffected. A gate leads directly from the coastal footpath to the interior of the service shed.

The roof of the shed is almost on a level with the surface of the swimming pool, and is treated as a continuation of the garden, being suitable for planting out with turf and shrubs. These two garden features, the roof-cum-garden and the pool, can be easily reached from anywhere in the house, and serve to blend the property into the coastal landscape.